HILLWALKS FROM THE SETTLE TO CARLISLE RAILWAY STATIONS

D1513325

DISCLAIMER

The author has taken all reasonable effort to ensure that the information herein is accurate, however the author accepts no responsibility if it is not, nor if unforeseen circumstances occur while doing the walk. We would also advise that in planning your walk you check local transport, accommodation and please be aware that some paths and rights of way may be affected by changes such as forestry work or weather. We would appreciate any information regarding changes. You can do this by contacting the Publisher in the first instance.

2QT Limited (Publishing)

First edition published 2013
2QT Limited (Publishing)
Lancaster
Lancashire LA2 8RE

www.2qt.co.uk

Cover design & typesetting by Dale Rennard
Photographs by Hugh and Margaret Stewart and David Reilly

Printed and bound in the UK by Berforts Information Press
The Printer uses FSC and PEFC accredited paper suppliers

A CIP catalogue record for this book is available
from the British Library
ISBN 978-1-908098-89-4

Hugh Stewart has spent most of his life repairing or replacing bits of folks' limbs as an orthopaedic surgeon, for the last twenty-three years in Lancaster and Kendal. Otherwise walking, climbing, cycling, and mountain biking cure the rage. This book is an addition to his first, "Settle to Carlisle, a Hillwalk", a long distance walk, published in 2010. He is married and lives near Lancaster.

ACKNOWLEDGEMENTS

Thanks to my wife Margaret for so many things: her encouragement; companionship; keen eye for interesting features on the walks; for grammatical corrections, and some photography.

Ian Tyler kindly informed us of the pony track off Roman Fell when we met him guiding at Scordale mines.

Steve Hastie and Matt Neale, Area Rangers for the Yorkshire Dales National Park Authority for the Three Peaks and Upper Wensleydale areas respectively, gave helpful advice about access and information about access as outlined in the section "Access".

Many thanks to "Frank" Walker for information about the caves and caving and also to David Reilly for providing some good quality photographs.

INTRODUCTION

The historic and iconic Settle to Carlisle Railway travels through some of the finest walking country of the Pennines, including the Craven limestone district around Settle, the Three Peaks area, Dentdale, Mallerstang and the upper Eden valley hills.

Historically, the presence of the railway popularised walks in this general area by allowing charter services for ramblers at the weekends, the Dales Rail service, starting in 1974 and becoming very popular. This persists today, the service starting in Blackpool and going via Blackburn to Settle on summer weekends. There are guided walks from most of the stations on the line every weekend, run by the Friends of Dales Rail, and separately by the Friends of the Settle-Carlisle Line, including buses laid on to extend the walking scope east and west. Only the outlines of these walks are given; to my knowledge the details are not published, but they are bound to be similar to most in this book.

There are good reasons for doing these walks: travelling entirely by train to and from a walk is, of course, somewhat greener than driving there, but even using a car to get to one station allows A to B walks without the use of two cars, and thus is greener. It also extends your scope, rather than just doing circular walks; using the train for all or part of your day's journey is certainly more relaxing and interesting than driving. But the main reason is that they are all cracking good walks.

Common sense suggests it is better, if driving to a station for a linear walk to another, to take the train first, rather than at the end, as then there is no time pressure and no waiting!

You will note that the walks are from the southern stations, because they are right in the midst of the hills, the distance of the hills from the stations increasing north of Garsdale. Hence there are no walks from stations north of Appleby here, but you can be consoled; there are other splendid books describing such walks, e.g. *Walking in Cumbria's Eden Valley*, by Vivienne Crow.

The walks are mainly "day" walks, going into the hills. As the majority of paths and ways up and round the hills are used, especially south of Kirkby Stephen, there is scope for making your own routes out of the ones outlined, to shorten, lengthen or just alter them to your liking. All the walks except one were worked out from maps and previous experience, although some will look very similar to other published walks. The only one I've pinched is from a book describing the River Lune catchment territory, *The Land of the Lune* by John Self, the circular walk from Dent Station over Blea Moor and Great Knoutberry Hill. It can't be improved.

Before each walk description the length, height climbed and time are given, which, along with the short description after these, should allow you to assess how hard a walk it is. The description of its difficulty is subjective, of course, and the time to do any walk individual; the time given is that which I and my wife, 60 year olds, took to do the walk, including a lunch stop and photographs. If you are new to the area, don't do the hardest first; see how you measure against the time and difficulties given of a walk without the words "hard" or "rough" in the description, and adjust the others accordingly. A graded list is also given to help you, after the main walk list.

It is important to note that although detailed descriptions of the routes are given, the ability to read the maps of the routes is vital, as is the use of a compass, which sometimes helps confirm the right direction, even in good visibility. In case you go astray the OS maps, as stated later, should be carried for good measure.

Interesting facts about features such as castles, antiquities, etc., which may be passed again on different walks, will generally be dealt with once, in the first walk encountered in the book, except where the route description is much shorter for a walk and the facts then fill out that chapter.

MAPS AND MAP REFERENCES

The OS 1:25,000 Explorer maps with Open Access Land marked give good detail, and just two, OL 2 and 19, are needed, unless you can't resist the Forest of Bowland excursion, when OL41 will be needed.

Map references given are the national grid ones, the system for which is explained at the edge of each OS map.

ACCESS

Every walk except one in this book uses either public rights of way or is on open access land, which is land designated by the Countryside and Rights of Way Act 2000 and enacted in 2005. Such land is outlined on the Explorer maps mentioned, which are entered and exited, as they should be, at official points.

Open access land allows you to walk but not cycle where you like, not just on paths. The owners are entitled to close the areas for any reason for 28 days a year, usually for grouse shooting, or fire risks, but must give warning. Ideally you should check the appropriate website before going on the walks. The general website is: http://www.naturalengland. org.uk/ourwork/enjoying/places/openaccess/default.aspx.

Dog walkers should have their dogs on short leads between 1st March and 31st July to minimise ground breeding bird disturbance, and also "in the vicinity of livestock". That means sheep, their protection from your dog, but my advice if cattle come after you plus dog is to let your dog go for your own safety.

The advice about boundaries is to "use gates, stiles or wall gaps in field boundaries where you can, as crossing walls hedges or fences can damage them". Fences are crossed in these walks, never with a risk of damaging them as they are easily stepped over, and one wall, with helpful extended stones like a stile.

The Yorkshire Dales National Park Authority have a map of stiles in the Park, if you wish to check in future (things change, hopefully websites are updated). It is found thus: http://www.yorkshiredales.org.uk/outandabout/rightsofwayandopenaccess/openaccessland/openaccess-gettingto.

The odd walk out is the Appleby circular walk into the Warcop Training area, which is not open access. It takes you off paths and is therefore done at your own discretion, and ONLY to be done when there is no shooting (see the notes of that walk).

Unfortunately the access to access land in certain areas, for whatever reason, is totally impractical. For example, there is a four mile northern border to the land north-east of Dent Station with no official exit to upper Wensleydale, which means that a logical and lovely continuation of the Widdale Fell ridge from Great Knoutberry Hill cannot be taken, and the wonderful gorge and waterfalls of Mossdale Gill cannot be visited satisfactorily. Perhaps this will change in future.

EQUIPMENT

Hill walking is potentially dangerous. Unless you are in a very settled period of high pressure, even in summer you should be prepared for rain, which along with wind can cause hypothermia if you are underdressed. Getting lost obviously lengthens the time that you will be cold and wet.

Hill walks involve mud and bog, so proper boots up to your ankles will stop most of the water getting in. In the unlikely event of a long dry period, walking shoes could be used. The only walk I wanted gaiters for was the Forest of Bowland one on a wet day, I find they irritate my skin.

Therefore the minimum you should take on the walks should be:

> this book
>
> the appropriate OS map and a compass and the knowledge of their usage
>
> waterproofs,
>
> an extra top layer and thin gloves.
>
> some food and drink.

MARILYNS, HEWITTS AND NUTTALLS

These walks are designed primarily for pleasure, not for hill bagging. However, as bagging seems to have become more and more popular, any Marilyns, Hewitts or Nuttalls visited in the routes will be noted by M, H and N respectively in the "summits visited" section at the start of each chapter.

John and Anne Nuttall started this in 1990, publishing walks to every hill over 2000 feet with a 50 feet drop on all sides. As the maps are metric the drop has been refined to 15 metres, (and 2000 feet is 610 metres). Alan Dawson refined this list to hills of 2000 feet height with the drop 30 metres (98 feet), calling them Hewitts in 1997. In 1992 he also compiled and published the list of Marilyns, a joke on the Munros of Scotland (Monroes), which is any hill with a drop of 150 metres on all sides, of any height.

Obviously every Hewitt is a Nuttall, but the Marilyns are separate and will be noted as such.

THE PENNINE BRIDLEWAY AND OTHER LONG DISTANCE PATHS

The walks in this book use the national long distance routes when appropriate, thus we meet the familiar names: the Ribble Way from Longton, on the tidal Ribble west of Preston, to Gavel Gap, which is passed on our Newby Head and Cam Fell circular walk; the Dales Way, from Ilkley to Bowness on Windermere: the Pennine Way from Edale to Kirk Yetholm; the Coast to Coast from St Bees to Robin Hood's Bay; and the Pennine Bridleway.

These are so common they will be abbreviated as follows:

Ribble Way:	RW
Dales Way:	DW
Pennine Way:	PW
Coast to Coast:	C to C
Pennine Bridleway:	PBW

Pennine Bridleway

This was the brilliant idea of Lady Mary Towneley, who in 1986 rode a horse between Derbyshire and Northumberland to highlight the state of the nation's bridleways and publicise the idea. Approval of a linked bridleway for horses, mountain bikes and walkers from Derbyshire to Cumbria, came in 1995, and in 2002 for an extension to Northumberland. Funded by Natural England, with a £1.8 million Sport England award to help, the southern section to the South Pennines was the first to open. The 52 miles in the Yorkshire Dales National Park (YDNP) was constructed by 2011, but agreement about access across the Settle to Carlisle line land was not finalised till June 2012 when the bridleway was opened by Martin Clunes at a ceremony at Far Moor Bridge, Selside. Funding has not been obtained for the final 141 miles from Street, near Ravenstonedale, to Byrness in

Northumberland, which would make the full "path" 347 miles long, although some of that distance includes the 47 mile Mary Towneley Loop in the south Pennines, a hard day's mountain biking I can tell you, and the ten-mile Settle Loop.

The itinerary is based on packhorse routes and old drove roads, "sensitively" upgraded, with some new paths created to link them up. Virtually every walk in this book south of Kirkby Stephen uses some of the bridleway, and it is in a generally excellent state, giving easy walking, unlike some of the older routes on the Mary Towneley Loop in the South Pennines.

Unfortunately Lady Towneley died in 2001, not living to see her superb idea come to full development.

CAVING

The western dales, through which the majority of the walks in this book pass, are naturally abounding in pot-holes and caves in the limestone bedrock, and even the northern walks outwith the Dales boundary all have areas of these limestone features.

I know nothing about the activity of caving/pot-holing, and have only been down into one wet cave, Gaping Gill, courtesy of the Craven Pothole Club's Bank Holiday winch. One impressive fact about the area I can tell you is that the "three counties system", centred on the Ease Gill and Bullpot area, which is slightly to the west of our walks, has over sixty miles of continuous underground "tunnels". You can enter in one of thirty entrances and theoretically pass from Cumbria under Lancashire into Yorkshire, or vice versa, although it would take days.

This is the largest system in the country, and the twenty-second largest in the world. The longest is 390 miles, in the USA of course, so the locals have a long way to go to be tops. China, I'm told, is the in place for new "digging".

The other interesting thing the exploration has shown is where drainage of one area goes to, which is not always as expected, and there other interesting facts about the odd pot/cave or two which will be pointed out in the text as they are encountered.

GOOGLE EARTH

I'm not a big fan of "the latest technology", and have a pet hatred of sat navs in cars, but have to recommend the use of Google Earth. Quite apart from helping me with planning, showing tracks and walls (sometimes), on open country, it is to be recommended to you, the walker, for use beforehand on certain walks to help in the location of some local earthworks, e.g. lynchets and pillow mounds, which can otherwise be hard to spot. Suggested use before a walk will be mentioned in the individual walk précis at the start of each chapter.

GEOLOGY

Most of the walks in the area are dominated by carboniferous limestone.

The ages of the periods referred to are shown:

The rocks will be discussed sequentially starting with the oldest:

Basement rocks

All the surface rocks of the Dales and Mallerstang are sedimentary, deposited by water, mostly under the sea. The oldest rocks are Silurian grits/slates, deposited

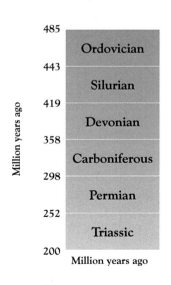

Million years ago	
485	Ordovician
443	Silurian
419	Devonian
358	Carboniferous
298	Permian
252	Triassic
200	

Million years ago

at the bottom of the Lapetus Ocean, which divided land roughly between what is now Scotland and England. This grit is exposed where two quarries produce it on the Quarries walk in Ribblesdale, with plenty more on the surface round the corner in Crummackdale, and the Norber Erratics are this rock. See the walk chapters for more explanation.

Carboniferous Limestone

The next layer, and the dominant rock of the area, gives rise to characteristic features. The Devonian desert was flooded by tropical seas, as our area was now a little south of the equator. The Yorkshire Dales National Park area roughly corresponds to what was a stable submarine plateau, called the Askrigg Block. This block is limited westwards by the Dent fault and southwards by the Craven fault. The stability of the block, and the fact that the seas were warm, shallow and clear, allowed deposition of shell debris which was pure. This is the pale grey limestone called Great Scar Limestone, up to 600 feet thick, most dramatically seen at Malham, but also around Attermire. The deposited beds were obviously horizontal, and remain so today, the lines between beds are bedding planes, caused by pauses in deposition. This limestone abounds with fossils.

Moughton unconformity, Horizontal limestone strata above off vertical Silurian grit. See Walk 4 for more details

Yoredale Series

"Yoredale" comes from Ure-dale, ie Wensleydale, where the layering effect of these sedimentary rocks, still of the Carboniferous period, are clearly seen along the sides. Large rivers came down from the north dropping mud and sand in the deltas formed on top of the Great Scar Limestone, and intermittent sea level rises with clear water gave further thin limestone beds. Thus these beds are layers of shale, sandstone and limestone, sometimes repeated, the weathering of which at uneven rates gives the characteristic stepped appearance of many of the hills here, i.e. the Three Peaks, as well as the sides of Wensleydale.

Within the shale layers of the Yoredale rocks there are occasional thin seams of coal, seen, e.g. on Fountains Fell and off the coal road, Garsdale, where pits existed.

Coal is formed by the partial decomposition and chemical conversion of large masses of organic matter. The matter first forms as peat, in stagnant water, then is covered by mineral deposition in seas as outlined above, this burial causing an increase in temperature and pressure to cause the conversion. The organic matter, evident by fossils in the layers above and below the coal, consisted of ferns, horsetails, club mosses and gymnosperms, the latter not including conifers, which developed later.

Millstone Grit

As the river deltas grew, the clear seas disappeared in the middle to upper Carboniferous period. The sands deposited by the deltas were coarse and had quartz pebbles in them, giving the characteristic rough dark sandstone called millstone grit, so called as circular stones, or querns, fashioned from it were used to grind corn. The Three Peaks, Fountains Fell, Wild Boar Fell and High Seat in Mallerstang are all capped with this rock, and there is obviously some on Nine Standards Rigg although the layer is not horizontal and therefore not a cap.

Igneous and other intrusions

At the end of the Carboniferous period, tectonic plate movement allowed the intrusion into the earth's crust of magma in what is now the northern Pennine region the crust here being the Yoredale series of limestones, shales and sandstones. On cooling, the magma crystallised and solidified into hard dolerite, the layer being maximally 230 feet thick. This is called The Great Whin Sill, as northern quarrymen called any hard dark rock, Whin, and any horizontal layer, Sill. The cooling caused vertical cracks to form, leading to the formation of polygonal columns, well seen on the sides of the magnificent High Cup. Dolerite is similar to basalt, but the crystals in basalt formed slower and hence were smaller, so basalt is smoother.

As the sedimentary rocks "dried out", they developed cracks, allowing movement of hot mineralised fluids into them in the Permian period. The liquids evaporated, leaving deposits of lead and copper and zinc, which were mined in parts of the area, detailed in the text.

Red Sandstone

In the Permian and Triassic periods, sand from dunes and rivers was deposited in a desert in what is now the Eden valley area, giving rise to the characteristic building stone north of Kirkby Stephen.

The Craven Faults

The southern Dales area has three fault lines running West to East, caused by earth movements in the late Carboniferous period. The north and south ones start from near Leck in the

Lune Valley territory, and the Mid-Craven one starts from the southeast end of Giggleswick Scar, running east through the line of Stockdale Lane (hence Attermire was formed by it) on to Malham Cove and Gordale Scar. The Mid-Craven Fault fractured the Carboniferous (Great Scar) limestone and raised the northern part between 600 and 3000 feet along its length, although time has eroded the edge to what you can see.

The north fault runs through Crummackdale, through Stainforth, where it helped with the two waterfalls seen on the Attermire walk, and on to Malham Tarn, where it helped bring impervious rocks to the surface and hence the Tarn formed.

North Pennine Escarpment
The basement rocks of the North Pennines are slates and volcanic rocks of the Ordovician and Silurian periods, like those of the Lake District, laid down as mud and volcanic ash on the edge of a wide ocean. They were then squashed and altered as the continents closed the ocean out, and a fault caused the eastern escarpment of the northern pennines, to the east of which these older rocks are exposed as a line of conical pikes, e.g. Knock, Dufton and Murton Pikes.

The effect of Ice Ages
Although the polar ice-cap has advanced and receded many times over many millions of years, it was the last one of four in the last sixty thousand years which was the most intense and wiped out most of the evidence of the previous ones. It finished about ten thousand years ago. Limestone pavements evident all over the area were caused first by the ice scouring vegetation and soil from the rock, and removing any irregularities by fracturing the rock along its horizontal bedding planes, to give a flat platform. The ice then deposited

soil or clay on the platform. Forests grew on this soil, causing mildly acidic water to seep down and erode the limestone along lines of vertical weakness. Thus blocks or clints were formed, separated by the eroded channels or grikes. The soil then slipped into the grikes and the remaining superficial soil eroded further not helped, it is thought, by man removing the forests.

Ice movements carried soil and boulders, dumping them as they thawed, sometimes as sheets, sometimes as egg-shaped mounds, sharp end forwards in the line of ice flow. These "drumlins" are seen all over the district, particularly around Ribblehead. Boulder deposition accounts for the Norber and other "erratics", further explanation in the text.

The classic "U" shaped valley caused by glacial erosion is High Cup Gill, best seen from the Nick.

You may see the word "karst" in many explanations of the region. This comes from a limestone area of former Yugoslavia, and means "bleak and waterless".

FLORA AND FAUNA

The hay meadows of the North Pennines are botanically profuse; the contrast between such a meadow and a heavily grazed area on the other side of a wall can be stark. Limestone grasslands and pavements are also characteristically lovely, particularly in the many nature reserves where sheep are excluded. On the moors different Alpine and Arctic flora species exist, especially where sheep can't get at them.

One of the delights of researching these walks has been in recognising the whereabouts of rare plants, which will be mentioned in each walk description, but this is in no way complete, as I have not been everywhere in every month.

The moors come alive with wading birds coming inland to

breed usually in late March, and you will see and hear the curlew and lapwing (peewit), and others I know little about. Red grouse are rarer in the heather moors than they used to be, but you will still disturb them, and if lucky may see a black grouse on the Abbotside Estate (Great Shunner Fell walk); where it is more likely than elsewhere you will see the rarer birds of prey, merlin and short eared owl. Hen harriers are now very rare; in 2012 only one pair tried to breed in England. Buzzards are the most common bird of prey, but peregrine falcons and even red kites are there.

Red squirrels live around Kirkby Stephen, particularly Smardale, also in Mallerstang and Garsdale/Widdale. Rabbits abound of course, but hares, foxes, roe deer and stoats can also be seen.

SETTLE

As the first six walks all go through parts of Settle, a bit about the town is in order.

It lies where the Craven fault crosses the River Ribble. The Craven fault divides the limestone country to the north and the grit stone hills to the south, and it has created the Aire gap or corridor, a through route from West Yorkshire to Lancaster, the Lakes or Western Dales. A turnpike was made here in 1753, the tollbooth being pulled down in 1820 to erect the Town Hall in its place. A bridge across the Ribble was not mentioned until 1498 however. The West Yorkshire to Lancaster railway also used this route, opening in 1847, and this led, of course, to the origins of the Settle to Carlisle railway in 1875, more about which later in this guide. Settle's heyday was in the 17th century, the activities of handloom weaving, stocking knitting and hat-making being prominent, and when surprisingly Settle was more important than Bradford or Sheffield! In the late 18th century cotton spinning became the main occupation, with five mills eventually working, powered by the waters of the Ribble.

It describes itself as a "bustling" market town on its website, and it certainly is on market day, Tuesdays, the market being in the central square.

A good view of the town can be had from the top of Castlebergh crag, a 50 foot limestone cliff recently bolted for the use of climbers. This is accessed by way of Constitution Hill, beside the Shambles. The Shambles is a three-storey building overlooking the market square, shops on two levels with houses above. Originally this was a butcher's and slaughterhouse in mediaeval times. A café on the south side of the square bears the name the Naked Man, with a carving and date above the door, which is interesting enough, but their home-made cakes cakes and bread alone are worth the visit.

There used to be a museum called charmingly the Pig Yard Club Museum housing remains from the nearby Victoria Cave, but it closed in the 1980s, the relics dispersed to the Leeds and British Museums and to private individuals. The cave was discovered on Queen Victoria's accession, hence the

Settle from Castlebergh

name, by a man whose dog disappeared down a foxhole. The current large entrance is man made. The oldest remains were dated at 130,000 years ago, when hyenas probably lived there, dragging bits of hippopotamuses and early rhinoceroses back to feast on. Successive layers of clay came as glaciers melted, and then about 11,000 years ago, brown bears hibernating, and the earliest evidence of human activity, a reindeer antler harpoon. Roman artefacts completed the top layer.

In 2009 an interesting community hydroelectric scheme opened, a 50 kW Archimedean screw alongside the fish ladder by the weir, seen from the car park of Bridge End Mill. Owned by the community to "empower" it, by residents taking responsibility for their future. It is designed to generate 165,000 kWh per year, i.e. to serve 50 average households per year. Costing £410,000, the estimated total annual income is £28,000. It is the first scheme in the country to get most of its income from selling electricity to the grid. A detailed report on the effect of salmon and other migrating fish concluded that no harm would be done, and the reduction of the flow through the fish ladder would actually ease the upward migration and even extend the migratory season. This seems to have encouraged others; a similar screw started in Bainbridge in mid 2011, "the first in the Yorkshire Dales National Park". Is that true? Yes it is; a little corridor of the Ribble here is outwith the Park.

THE WALKS

FROM, THE STATIONS OF:

SETTLE

		Distance (Miles)	Ascent (Feet)	Time (Hours)
1	Malham circular	13.5	2600	6
2a	Attermire, Catrigg Force, Stainforth circular	8.3	1677	3 ½
2b	Attermire, Victoria and Jubilee caves.	4.7	1294	2
2c	Attermire, V and J caves, Winskill	6.7	1446	2 ½
3	Settle to Horton-in-Ribblesdale via Fountains Fell	13.5	2516	6 ½
4	Settle to Horton-in-Ribblesdale via the Celtic Wall and Moughton	9.1	1838	4 ½
5	Settle to Ribblehead via Norber and Ingleborough.	14.5	2930	8
6	Bowland circular via Gisburn Forest, Knotteranum and Bowland Knotts.	15.1	1897	7 ½

HORTON-IN-RIBBLESDALE

		Distance (Miles)	Ascent (Feet)	Time (Hours)
7	Penyghent.	8.9	1913	4
8	Horton to Ribblehead via Ingleborough and Simon Fell.	12.2	2381	5 ½
9	Horton circular via the Quarries and Norber.	9.8	1305	4 ½

RIBBLEHEAD

		Distance (Miles)	Ascent (Feet)	Time (Hours)
10	Whernside via Greensett.	8	1692	4
11	Bruntscar, Chapel-le-Dale, Gauber circular.	7.7	722	3
12	Dent Station via Whernside, its tarns and Dentdale	8.9	2194	4
13	Newby Head and Cam Fell circular.	12.2	1728	5

GRADED DIFFICULTY LIST OF WALKS

Taking distance, ascent and the ground conditions into account.
You may disagree.

Stations started from given after names:

S: Settle; H: Horton-in-Ribblesdale; R: Ribblehead; D: Dent;
G: Garsdale; KS: Kirkby Stephen; A: Appleby.

		Distance (Miles)	Ascent (Feet)	Time (Hours)
1	11. Bruntscar, Chapel-le-Dale, Gauber Circular. R	7.7	722	3
2	2b. Attermire, Victoria and Jubilee Caves. S	4.7	1294	2
3	2c. Attermire, V and J Caves, Winskill. S	6.7	1446	2 ½
4	2a. Attermire, Catrigg Force. Stainforth circular. S	8.3	1677	3 ½
5	22. Smardale circular, return via Ash Edge. KS	11	1595	4 ½
6	9. Horton circular via the Quarries and Norber. H	9.8	1305	4 ½
7	4. Settle to Horton-in-Ribblesdale via the Celtic Wall and Moughton. S	9.1	1838	4 ½
8	7. Penyghent. H	8.9	1913	4
9	10. Whernside via Greensett. R	8	1692	4
10	12. Dent Station via Whernside, its tarns and Dentdale. R	8.9	2194	4
11	13. Newby Head and Cam Fell circular. R	12.2	1728	5
12	14. Blea Moor and Great Knoutberry Hill circular. D	10.8	2230	5
13	16. Rise Hill/Aye Gill Pike and Dentdale circular. D	12.7	1968	6

SETTLE

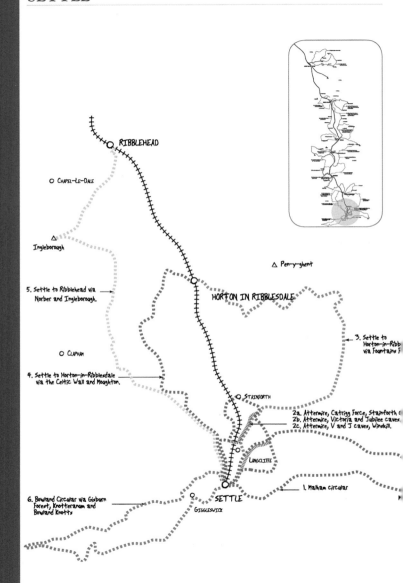

RIBBLEHEAD

○ Chapel-le-Dale

△ Ingleborough

△ Pen-y-ghent

HORTON IN RIBBLESDALE

5. Settle to Ribblehead via Norber and Ingleborough.

○ Clapham

3. Settle to Horton-in-Ribb via Fountains F

4. Settle to Horton-in-Ribblesdale via the Celtic Wall and Moughton.

○ Stainforth

2a. Attermire, Catrigg Force, Stainforth
2b. Attermire, Victoria and Jubilee caves.
2c. Attermire, V and J caves, Winskill.

Langcliffe

6. Bowland Circular via Gisburn Forest, Knotteranum and Bowland Knotts

SETTLE

Giggleswick

1. Malham circular

1. MALHAM CIRCULAR

Start and finish: Settle Station
13.5 miles   2600 ft. ascent   6 hours
Summits: none
Google Earth: shows the lynchets around Malham

A longish walk but with long stretches of easy walking, limestone country mostly. Two steep sections up from Settle and at Malham Cove, and a fairly steep grassy descent to Malham. Attermire Crags to admire on the way, the impressive Malham Cove to look forward to after tea or a pub stop in Malham. Easy walking back, with views of the Three Peaks and then the Ribble valley. It is based on the Settle Loop of the PBW, although that does not extend to Malham for some reason. Done anti-clockwise for the views of the Cove. Wild flowers in profusion in spring and summer.

From the station go down to the main road, Station Road, and turn right into the town. At the top turn left on the main street, cross it via the pedestrian crossing and turn right up Chapel Street.

> **The Folly**
> At the top of Chapel Street is an impressive 17th century building, The Folly, now the Museum of North Craven Life. If time permits this is worth a visit, if for no other reason than to see the Settle to Carlisle railway model (part of) on the top floor.

Carry on past the Folly up Victoria Street, which becomes cobbled. Keep left at the first junction following the signs to Kirkby Malham and Airton, and at the next junction fork

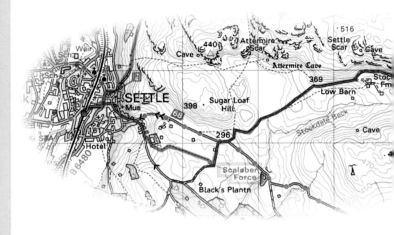

right, signposted "The Pinfold 150 yards", and also "Pennine Bridleway", the Settle Loop of which you will be on most of today.

Eighty yards after the road swings right, turn left up a track signposted "Lamberts Lane 1 mile". A small circular PBW sign is on the post although the PBW actually continues up the road to Lamberts Lane. The track climbs quite steeply to the corner of a wood by a reservoir, over a stile or through a gate, and then curves left up the field to go through a gap in the wall at the top, alongside which there is a small gap stile. The maps show the path going sharp left just past the reservoir and then sharp right by the top wall, but this is obviously not necessary.

Thirty yards past the gap in the wall, go over a stile in the wall on the right and follow this wall round to the left on a green path/track, crossing one wall by a step style to enter Lamberts Lane by a gate, where a sign indicates "Settle 1.25". Turn left up the lane, right at the Settle/Malham road, and

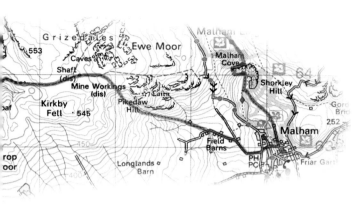

after a hundred yards turn left onto Stockdale Lane. This is metalled all the way to Stockdale Farm, so just follow the tarmac, observing and admiring the various caves and crags of Attermire Scar on the left. Stockdale Lane is on the line of the Mid Craven Fault (see "Geology") with limestone to your left and the grit and shale scenery to your right.

As you see the farm on the right, the tarmac road deviates to the farm but you have to be careful to go left onto a path marked for the PBW, part stony and part grassy to give the feet a rest.

Attermire

3

At the gate opposite Kirkby Fell on your right, the path has been made up, and at the next gate, Nappa Gate, the PBW turns off left, but you carry straight on, signposted "Cove Road."

Pikedaw Hill Mines
The mine workings that you may see evidence of around here and on the path down to Malham are of a calamine (zinc oxide) mine, although some lead was also produced. Mineral workings such as this are characteristic of fault lines, and we are still on the Mid Craven. The caverns, extending 3000 feet in total, are natural, and were explored in the 18th and 19th century for the minerals via two entrance shafts, and rediscovered for potholers in 1944, the entrance a metal-lidded 70 foot vertical shaft, just to the north of the path past Nappa Gate.

Malham Tarn
The tarn is an oddity, the highest lake in England, and only one of eight alkaline lakes in Europe. The fact that it is here at all, in porous limestone country, seems odd; it was formed by glacial meltwaters after the last ice age, lying on a bed of impervious Silurian rock overlaid by boulder clay. Now Silurian rock is much older than carboniferous limestone, so should be underneath it, and I can't explain that further except to say that faults can do funny things, and the North Craven Fault is just south of the Tarn. The outflow travels 500 or 600 yards and then disappears at "Water Sinks" and does not appear under Malham Cove as you might imagine, but at Aire Head, south of the village.

Malham Tarn now appears over to the left. After 350 yards a signpost indicates a path on the right, "Malham 1.5 miles", which you must take. A glorious view now unfolds of the

Craven area north of Skipton. The narrow path steepens and winds its way down to go over a step-stile in a wall. From here you see a clear line of barns ahead which is the line of your route. At the next wall there is a choice of gate or step-stile. At the bottom of the next field, after crossing a small stream in front of a barn, go through a gate, or a small gated step-stile to its right, and head down towards where the stream on your right meets a wall at the bottom. Cross the stream on a two-sleeper bridge and head towards the barn, in front of which is a track, which you enter through a gate. Turn left, a signpost indicates Malham, and cross the stream again via a limestone slab. The 260 foot high limestone cove now comes into view.

As you descend the lane further, turn right at the junction with Long Lane and look across the valley

Warrendale Knotts

Malham Cove and cows

Towards Malhamdale

towards the northwest. To the left of the entrance to Gordale Scar you will see striking evidence of ancient field systems, longitudinal terraces or lynchets down the fields. The map marks them somewhat north of what you can see.

> **Lynchets**
> Lynchet is the diminutive of lynch, meaning an agricultural terrace. Deliberate terracing seems to me to be a much better explanation for the features seen across the valley, rather than the classic one that they are banks formed by the effect of ploughing on a slope over a long period of time, as large areas are taken up by them. They are thought to be of mediaeval origin.

Long Lane then turns left, and at a T-junction with another lane turn left and then after 20 yards turn right down an enclosed path/lane, which leads you onto Cove Road and the Beck Hall tea shop magically in front over the "Moon" clapper bridge (after its builder), where you can see if the ducks still like clotted cream. Or you can turn right for pub refreshment.

After recharging, carry on the line of the bridge up a path, turning sharp left at the top onto a lane, and then through a kissing gate onto a path. A sign tells you there is no access from here to the top of Malham Cove this side of the river. I can tell you that if

you ascended the steep hillside to what is called the right wing of the Cove, climbers from here have

Lynchets seen from the west

never been deterred from hopping over the fence and onto the path leading to the Malham Rakes road, as that is the nearest parking for them.

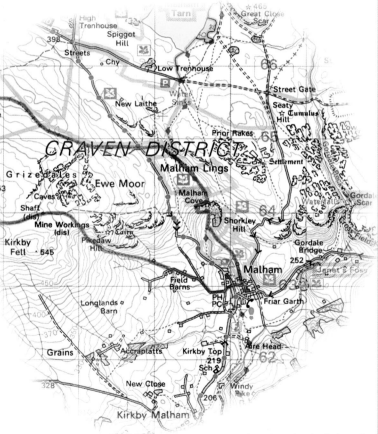

However, you are going for a close-up of the majestic Cove, so carry on along the excessively well-marked path (they don't want anyone to stray off it or pinch the rocks), till you descend a short steep bank, where you head left to the clapper bridge, not right through a gate stile. If you look across left to the path on the other side, the hordes of tourists, and on weekdays school groups, will persuade you that your way from Malham has been the better one.

> **Malham Cove**
> A magnificent 260 foot high, 300 yard wide concave sheer cliff of carboniferous limestone, overhanging in its central part. Formed by the Mid Craven Fault, which lies about 600 yards south, erosion has eaten it northwards, particularly by glacial meltwater pouring over the lip. This isn't entirely logical, however, as the dry valley of Watlowes, down which the meltwaters flowed, is clearly much narrower than the Cove. Another mystery. Nevertheless, the explanation given for the concavity of the Cove is that the central flow was greater than the peripheral.
>
> The stream emanating from the base arises from the area of the smelt mill chimney sinks, southwest of the Tarn, not the tarn outflow as explained under "Malham Tarn".

You will inevitably see climbers here, unless it is freezing, as it is an internationally recognised crag, and a "winter sunshine" crag, ie it traps the sun and warms the fingers when other, less sheltered crags are unclimbable. There are 242 recorded routes on the UKC website, with the classic ones (traditional, relying on placing your own protection) to each wing, and the extreme ones in the central part, relying on permanent bolts for protection.

Across the river, turn right then left up the steps to ascend to the left of the Cove. I counted 404 steps till just beyond the wicket gate at the top. The last digit is correct, although you could argue about what is a step, but the middle digit may be out as it gets a bit tedious remembering the tens, which means the first digit may be one out too!

At the top, wander over the limestone pavement, scoured clean of vegetation by the last glacier here, or the grassy bank higher up if you fear for your ankles, to take in the phenomenon if you haven't trod this way before.

At the far end turn left up the dry valley called Watlowes, and continue along it and up steps at the end and across a wooden style, continuing straight on, signed "Langscar Gate", not right as most walkers doing the Malham classic circuit and PW will do.

Careful though, as 20 yards further on you must go up and over a ladder stile on the left, on the other side of which a sign tells you that Langscar Gate is 300 yards away. Which is partly why I am writing in yards, not metres.

Malham Cove

At Langscar Gate, cross the road and go through the gate with a no motorcycle or car sign on it, but with the sign post indicating a byway open to all traffic, "Cow Close Langcliffe 4 miles"!

Watlowes

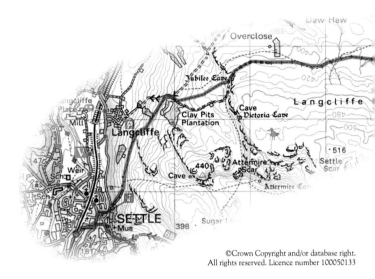

After a few hundred yards of grassy track you will notice you are back on the PBW, joining from the south where you left it this morning. It will now be obvious that it is a loop from Settle, although not marked as such until the far end.

The track is very likeable, the cattle have obviously found it so, but as you enter the National Trust land at SD875652 the track has been renovated and the mud is behind you. Rapid progress can now be made, just as well as the moorland scenery, probably with gritstone bedrock, something to do with being on the North Craven Fault, is a bit drab to start with. But soon Ingleborough, with Whernside to its right appears behind the mass of Fountains Fell, and later Penyghent further right.

Watch out for lesser spearwort in the ditches on the left, which you may take for buttercups at first.

As you eventually come round a corner into limestone crag scenery, with the small Jubilee Cave on the left and a gate

on the track in the distance, if you prefer to give your feet a rest, go over the ladder stile on the right and follow the grassy path down, aiming for the wood half left.

> **Jubilee Cave**
> Three entrances, connected if you can squeeze through a narrow fissure from left to central, and less of a squeeze to the right one.

This path regains the track at the wood; go through the gate and down the track to join the road coming over from Malham Tarn, where immediately turn left through a gate, a signpost indicating the PBW in three directions, now explaining that you have been on the subsidiary Settle Loop.

Ingleborough from Langcliffe Scar track

The obvious path takes you gently down to Settle; when you hit the lane near the bottom watch out for a sign inside some wooden gates indicating the way to Castlebergh through some private woods. The view of Settle from the top of this cliff is the best around, although the climb through the woods may not be tempting after six hours of walking.

Further down, either go direct to the station by going left by the short blue "PBW" sign, down into a cobbled lane, past Lloyds bank where you turn right to the main road, or go straight on at the "PBW" sign to the market place if you haven't looked round Settle before, and various cafés/teashops, including a Naked Man, or call in at the Lion on the main street for something more perky before your train. Cheers.

Penyghent from Langcliffe Scar track

2a. ATTERMIRE, CATRIGG FORCE, STAINFORTH CIRCULAR

Start and finish: Settle Station
8.3 miles.   1677 ft. ascent.
3½ hours, plus any for cave exploration.
Summits: none
Google Earth: of no special use.

Easy walking in limestone terrain, several caves worth a visit, particularly Victoria Cave, so take a torch. Impressive waterfall in Catrigg Force, easy walk back via the RW by the Ribble.

This walk started as a summer kiddy walk for us many years ago, 4.7 miles just Attermire via a circuit, then it graduated to a 6.7 miles January afternoon walk via Winskill and Stackhouse, and has now lengthened for this book. It can be shortened as indicated and the shortened walks will be given at the end of this chapter, called B for the 4.7 mile and C for the 6.7 mile walk.

From the station go down to the main road, Station Road, and turn right into the town. At the top turn left on the main street, and onto Market Square on the right. Go up the far side of Market Square to Constitution Hill, which curves to the left. Soon after note the wooden gates on the right, not signed at all but they give access to Castlebergh Crag, a short walk up through the private wood with permissive access which gives a splendid view of Settle.

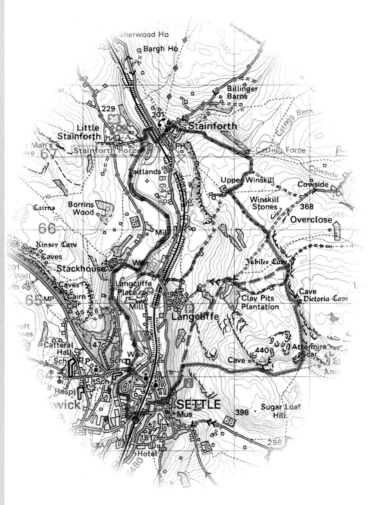

Route 2a
Route 2b
Route 2c

Just past these gates the way splits; take the right hand track, Banks Lane, signposted "Pennine Bridleway, Langliffe 1½" .Just after the first gate by a ruined building on the left fork right up the steep field on an obvious path, although you can see the signpost for this path a hundred yards further on

The ascent to Attermire, from Giggleswick

by a wall. Past the next ruined wall turn up the hill on whichever path takes your fancy, off the main path which appears to carry on diagonally. Higher up, the path comes alongside a wall by a ruined trough; keep going up. Go through the next wall by a small gate or large

Attermire scar and cave

one, and a hundred yards further on the path divides, only to rejoin after the "Cave" of Warrendale Knotts, seen on the left by a gap in a wall. It therefore matters not which path you take. At the bottom of the next field there is usually a pool in front of the ladder stile you have to negotiate, except in very dry weather. Some small stones by the wall should help you out.

Admire the wild west scenery of Warrendale Knotts on the left, really Torrs rather than the usual cliff pattern, and try to ignore the scruffy remains of what Wainwright called an old rifle range target on your right.

Route 2a

Route 2b

The path now climbs up and round to the left through a natural gap, joining a wall on the right and then through it by a small gate. For a short while the path has been upgraded, but is easy going anyway, and when it levels out it gives good views of Ingleborough, with its long north ridge to the right, and Whernside beyond the end part of the ridge.

After a kissing gate you will see Victoria Cave as a defect in the scar up to the right, and an oblique path leads up to it. It is well worth a visit with a torch, and the able-bodied will be able to go to the back left of the cave and up a slope to emerge into daylight.

Victoria Cave

The cave was discovered on Queen Vic's accession, hence the name, by a man whose dog disappeared down a foxhole, probably the one I have alluded to in the text, up and to the left of the main entrance. The current large entrance is man made. The oldest remains were dated at 130,000 years ago, when hyenas probably lived there, dragging bits of hippopotamuses and early rhinoceroses back to feast on. Then successive layers of clay came as glaciers melted and then, about 11,000 years ago, brown bears hibernating, and the earliest evidence of human activity, a reindeer antler harpoon. Roman artefacts completed the top layer.

Another diagonal path leads down north back to the main path; note the accessible slit of the aptly named Wet Cave on the way down. The path ends at a kissing gate, and onto a track. Carry on up this to the right for two hundred yards, and over a ladder stile in the wall on the left. Go down the path for twenty yards (note here Walk B carries straight on) and then right on a path which curves round under the fragmented scar, over a ladder stile at the next wall, then half left to cross a path from the Malham Tarn area, to curve round right and join the Langcliffe to Malham Tarn road. Turn right over the cattle grid, being careful that the sudden view of Penyghent doesn't distract you from ending up in it, and a little way further on turn left down a track signed "Pennine Bridleway Stainforth 1¾". The track is metalled to the Winskill farms; the first farm is "Upper" on the map, "High" on the gate.

A perfect but single erratic of Silurian rock is obvious

Winskill erratic, both Winskills, and Ingleborough

Warrendale Knotts

Victoria cave

Route 2a
● ● ● Route 2c

on the right a way down, on its limestone base. (see Walk number 8 for explanation of erratics). Just before whatever Winskill farm it is, turn right before the cattle grid on a green track signed "Pennine Bridleway 1¾". I could have sworn we've just walked ½ mile! (Note here Walk C leaves to the left.)

After a gate and a gateway the track curves to the right and joins another obvious track at a T junction; turn left onto this and through the gate with a PBW sign on it.

Down this track and through a small gate on the right signed "Catrigg Force" only, the waterfall and glen being worth a visit. The force is on the line of the North Craven Fault, as is the smaller Stainforth Force in the Ribble.

Back at the lane, Goat Scar Lane or "Gooseker" locally,

go down to Stainforth, admiring the curious shape of Smearsett Scar in the distance. In the village at the green, go to the right and across the easy stepping stones over Stainforth Beck. This was the site of a "stoney ford", i.e. Stainforth. Go left, at the road junction

Catrigg Force

look at the small yard on the left "Piggery or Pinfold", and either go left to the Craven Heifer for sustenance then down to the main Settle to Horton-in-Ribblesdale road via the public toilets in the car park, or if you prefer to visit churches, keep right here for St Peter's, built only in 1842, prior to which the faithful had to go to Giggleswick, in whose parish they were.

> **The Craven Heifer**
> You may have noticed, if you are not from Yorkshire, an extraordinary number of inns and pubs with this name throughout the west and north of the county. The heifer was a very large specimen, weighing 312 stone and 8lbs, and her length was 11 feet and 4 inches. She was bred by the Reverend Carr in 1807 on the Duke of Devonshire's estate, and was admired by all until her end in 1812, won as a bet in a cockfight!

At the car park by the main road, head towards the beck and find the PBW path again, which passes under the main road into a picnic area and turns right, to join a track from the main road. Turn left on this over the railway and follow the PBW signs right, along the top of the railway embankment. At the lane turn left to Little Stainforth. The lane, an old monastic route, crosses the Ribble by a lovely packhorse bridge.

> **Stainforth Bridge**
> You can't see it, but upstream of here there used to be a water mill, originally a corn mill, and then for the cotton industry in the first half of the 19th century. In fact there were two water mills at that time. The bridge was built in 1675, and since 1931 has been owned by the National Trust, as a plaque on the south parapet proudly displays.

Stainfoth stepping stones

Just over the bridge turn left on the path marked Stackhouse, to go by the Ribble and very soon the Stainforth Force, in fact a smallish waterfall, but a delightful spot with a deep pool down stream of the fall, in which it is "strongly recommended" that you don't swim. In autumn salmon are said to be seen jumping up the falls. This is a honey pot though; you are unlikely to get a photo without other folk in it.

The path is now very obvious and no detailed description is necessary, except to say that after the first stile, which can be bypassed as the fence is currently down, do not go down to the river unless you want a boggy reascent to the next stile; contour round as the map indicates.

At present, 2011, the mill over the Ribble halfway to Langcliffe is being dismantled and is not a pretty sight, but things soon improve and at the weir and footbridge turn right

Stainforth bridge

on a narrow lane signed "Stackhouse". (Walk C joins here.) Turn left at the road and admire the quiet hamlet of Stackhouse. Two hundred yards after the wood on the right has ended, turn left down a path marked "Ribble Way Settle Bridge ¾". This leads easily down to the river again and past playing fields to Settle Bridge, where left for the town and refreshments or jollity, or keep straight on for the station on the RW.

Turn over the Ribble at the next footbridge down and follow the lane right round Kings Mill flats, then left up a track signposted halfway up as a cycle/walkway, to join a road by the fire station. Turn right here and shortly right again up a path to Booths' carpark, carrying on past Booths' entrance, then a school on your left, turning left on the road past the school for the station under the bridge and right.

2b. ATTERMIRE, VICTORIA AND JUBILEE CAVES
4.7 miles.   1294 ft. ascent.   2 hours.

As for route A till after the stile near Jubilee Cave, where carry straight on the path where the above walk turns right. The path lead down and regains the track at the wood; go through the gate and down the track to join the road coming over from Malham Tarn, where immediately turn left through a gate. An interesting sign post here indicates the PBW in three directions.

The obvious path takes you gently down to Settle, where you simply retrace your steps.

▬▬▬ Route 2a
▬ ▬ ▬ Route 2b

2c. ATTERMIRE, VICTORIA AND JUBILEE CAVES, WINSKILL
6.7 miles. 1446 ft. ascent. 2½ hours

As for route A till Upper or High Winskill, where go left on a lane, immediately over a cattle grid. Round the corner go over a gated stile on the left signed "Langcliffe 1". The obvious path crosses a field, and after the next stile (or gate, there are both) the path turns right and descends by the wall, down a steep hawthorn studded bank. After the next gate there is a further short descent then a more gradual descent to the left, eventually ending up on an enclosed lane.

As you approach Langcliffe, note a signpost on the right by a stile and a gate, indicating the way back to Stainforth, but you must take the path on the right immediately after this by

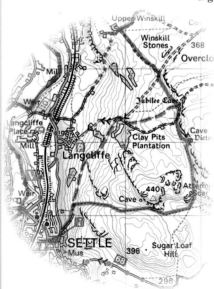

a gate, which descends between a wall and a fence to a track in front of the railway line. Turn left on this, right at the road, over the railway by a separate hardwood footbridge, cross the road and go straight down the minor road to the houses by the weir. A large millpond for Langcliffe Mill is seen on the left, and a fish ladder by the weir.

Cross the footbridge and join the end of the parent route.

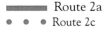 Route 2a
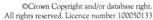 Route 2c

3. SETTLE TO HORTON-IN-RIBBLESDALE VIA FOUNTAINS FELL

Start: Settle Station
Finish: Horton-in Ribblesdale Station
13.5 miles   2516 ft. ascent.   2247 ft. descent.   6½ hours.
Summits: Fountains Fell, 2192 ft., 668m., (M,H);
Fountains Fell South Top, 2172ft., 662m., (N).

A long but straightforward walk, the main fell is gritstone moorland, but the introduction and ending are on limestone terrain. The summit plateau has many obsolete industrial features.

From the station go down to the main road, Station Road, and turn right into the town. At the top turn left on the main street, and onto Market Square on the right. Go up the far side of Market Square to Constitution Hill, which curves to the left. Soon after note the wooden gates on the right, not signed at all but they give access to Castlebergh Crag, see Walks 1 and 2.

Just past these gates the way splits, take the right hand track, Banks Lane, "Pennine Bridleway, Langcliffe 1½". Carry on as the lane opens out to go alongside the wall on the left, till nearly past the small wood down the slope, where go left over a ladder stile, or a gate ten yards further on, to carry on in the same line to another gate just to the right of a copse. Carry on by the wall, the path soon turning downhill through a gate and descending steeply to Langcliffe.

Cross the car park in Langcliffe and follow the lane marked "Stainforth 1½ miles". The lane leads pleasantly through

MALHAM CIRCULAR

the village and then between fields, before opening out to a path and gently climbing alongside the wall on the right at first, eventually steeply to a gate. Go up the bank through hawthorns, to pass through a wide gap between walls to a stile or gate on the left. Cross the next field climbing to a gated stile over a wall, a few yards to the left of a telegraph pole with a box on it. In the lane turn right, to round a corner and cross a cattle grid by Upper (map) or High (signed) Winskill.

Carry straight on along a green track signed "Pennine Bridleway Stainforth 1¾". After a gate then a gateway, the track curves to the right and joins another obvious track at a T junction; turn left onto this and through the gate signed "Pennine Bridleway Stainforth". Around now you can see the full extent of the "ridge" of Fountains Fell you will soon be climbing; it doesn't look terribly exciting but you will enjoy it on a clear day.

Down the track and through a gate, there is a small gate on the right signed Catrigg Force only. The waterfall and glen are worth a visit, see Walk 2.

Back up from the Force, go left, just north of east, through a gate separated from the one you came through from

Winskill by a wall, to follow that wall for 100 yards or so and then right over a ladder stile signed "Henside Road 1½". Climb the bank in line with the sign, to cross another ladder stile in a wall, well to the left of the crest of the hill. Note that if you did not want to visit the Force today, and

Langcliffe

24

hence did not feel the need to go down then up this bank, simply take a line alongside the wall at the top of the bank to this stile, although note also that the field is private land.

Carry on in the same line to join a green track from the right, which goes down to cross the Cowside Beck by a ford, but you can use the bridge. Follow the track up the bank till some conifers appear ahead, aim to the right of these to cross a wall by a gated stile. Carry on parallel to the wall, and if the gate at the end on the right where the walls meet is open, use this or the ladder stile to gain a short track to the road. This is shorter than the path marked on the map which goes through a gate by some trees, then right over a stile and back to the road across a field.

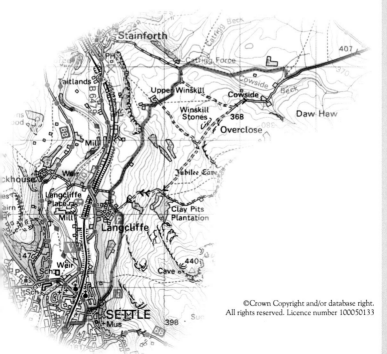

On the minor road turn left. For ¾ mile you must plod uphill with no great floral displays on the banks. Sorry: got to be done. At the T junction with Henside Road go straight ahead through the gate onto the moor by a sign, "Bridleway Arncliffe road 2 miles", onto a small but obvious path. This leads past a small quarry, up a slope and comes to a wall at a stile. Stay on this side of the wall heading left, i.e. east of north, and you soon join a tractor or quad track which leads gently up the hill, with views of Malham Tarn soon coming into view.

> **Fountains Fell**
> Named after the Cistercian monks of Fountains Abbey 25 miles to the east, who owned it and used it for sheep grazing, it is the 23rd highest hill in the Yorkshire Dales National Park. The same as the other Yorkshire Dales fells, it is has a limestone base, with Yoredale shales and sandstones above this, in which there are, or certainly were, poor coal seams, and it is capped by a layer of Grassington grit. The coal was of poor quality and is supposed to have been mined in Roman times, but certainly was from 1790 to 1860, the coal being used for lead smelting. A coke oven, or igloo as Wainwright calls it, is evident on the plateau for this use.

As you approach a trig point (593 on the map), you can either cross the broken down wall and then the (sometimes electric) fence by a helpfully built pile of stones, to follow its left side upwards, or continue on the right side of it and a broken wall for 500 yards till a gate allows access to the left side, just past another broken down wall. The terrain now turns into gritstone type moorland, with peat hags, but the track weaves its way nicely between the obstacles. The wall continues to be of limestone though, until much higher up.

Where the broken wall turns left, westwards, at SD870700, cross over it and follow a path on its right side, posts

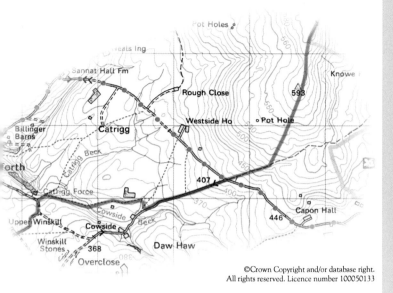

marking the way irregularly. This ensures that you will pass over Fountains Fell south top, a Nuttall, if you're interested, although it's not marked. The wall becomes solid, and hence potentially damageable if climbed, at the right-angled bend in it just south of this top. The path on the right also leads directly to the main summit cairn, leaving the wall just past Fountains Fell Tarn. However, in poor visibility it would be better to keep to the left of the wall, up to near the south top, then down slightly, until you pass to the right through the

Fountains Fell from Catrigg

27

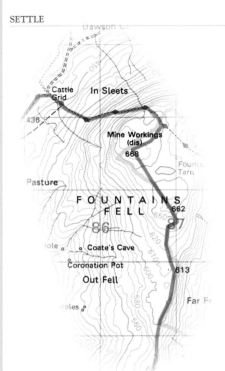

Mine shaft in Fountains Fell

wall at a wall junction, by a solid wood gate, then up to the cairn on the right.

From the summit cairn, head towards the stone building you see to the northeast, the path soon leading to an old sunken track which curves round banks, but not two bogs, which have to be negotiated before the coke oven building is reached. Beyond this there is an impressive fenced off circular shaft that can be visited. The constructed PW path is soon met; turn left on it to visit another shaft and the two large cairns if you wish, then cross the wall stile and down the wide path, at first gently and then steeper as it turns obliquely left down the hill, among some small gritstone outcrops. This track was the original access to the coal pits on the summit. Continue down to the road.

The Old Pennine Way

It is unfortunate that the dotted line on the map leading leftwards 200 yards from the road is not a path you can use to minimise road walking, as it is long disused; it was the official Way at the start in 1964, but at least by 1967 when Wainwright wrote his *Pennine Way Companion* it was a boggy mess and he recommended the road instead. I don't know what the dots are mean't to represent in any case, as they are too big for a path, and too small for a parish boundary.

Turn left down the road for nearly a mile, till just past a cattle grid where turn right down the track of the PW. At Dale Head farm curve to the right, white signs "PW" on a wall help, and continue till just past the impressive hole of Churn Milk Hole. Here turn left towards "Helwith Bridge". Ignore the path signed to the left after a short while, keep on the track through a gate in a wall and swing right. Excellent end-on views of Penyghent to the right, and also, unfortunately, of Horton Quarry across the valley, showing just how much of Yorkshire they have taken so far.

The Pennine Way off Fountains Fell

Penyghent from the south

29

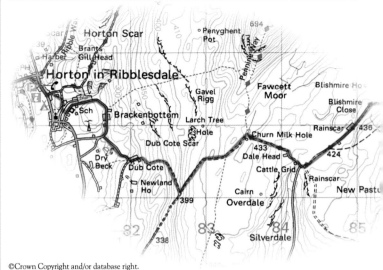

As the track descends, the impressive low linear Hayber Hill appears down to the right.

> **Hayber Hill**
> At first this might appear to be a perfect Drumlin, ie a glacial deposit, one of many in Ribblesdale. However, they should have a blunter leading end, ie the north end, which it doesn't, both ends being tapered nicely. I can find no information on it. All the rocks evident on its slopes are limestone, by the way.

Before the next crossing wall; turn sharp right down a path signed "Dub Cote ¾ mile", but don't follow it when it goes through a gate at the next wall, instead go down left here to a ladder stile over the bottom wall. A track leads down to Dub Cote, where there is a bunkhouse by the road junction. Turn down the road, and to avoid the main road, turn right at the next junction, past Brackenbottom, down through a pleasant wood to cross the Douk Ghyll by a footbridge just past the school. Turn right back upstream and shortly left up a track which connects to the PW track from Penyghent.

Hayber Hill, Ingleborough beyond

If you want some grass underfoot a very thin wall stile exists some way past the farm gate on the left, easily missed. It is just before a wire fence starts on top of the wall, and the path goes up to the corner of the wall round the house then down to the right at the bottom , to join the PW lane just before the house, by a poor stile. Go down to the main road, turn right, calling either at the Penyghent Café or the Crown en route to the station, up a final slope I'm afraid.

4. SETTLE TO HORTON-IN-RIBBLESDALE VIA THE CELTIC WALL AND MOUGHTON

Start: Settle Station
Finish: Horton-in-Ribblesdale Station
9.1 miles.   1838 ft. ascent.   1542 ft. descent.   4½ hours.
Summit: Moughton, 1402 ft., 427m.
Google Earth: shows the Celtic Wall,
which is not marked on maps.

A moderate walk on limestone pasture mostly, with many stiles to negotiate. The mystifying Celtic wall is visited and the geological oddity of Crummackdale. Moughton is not a place to visit for the first time in bad visibility, although it can be bypassed safely.

Go down to Station Road and turn left under the railway. About 150 yards past the turning on the right after the school a signed footpath goes right, past the back of the school and conveniently (if you need provisions) right onto the front of Booths' supermarket. The path continues in the same line beyond Booths' carpark and soon joins a road. Turn left and just after the fire station turn left onto the

Celtic Wall, Smearsett Scar and Penyghent

footpath/cycleway. This leads to a lane, leading round right, and past Kings Mill flats. Past this you see the river Ribble on the left, cross this by the bridge and turn right on the Ribble Way, leading pleasantly past Settle College, a 13 to 19 comprehensive, to cross the main road.

Carry on here on the enclosed path between playing fields, and after a short dogleg and a gated stile, the next field is crossed on an obvious open path. Two more stiles and you are on a wooded bank above the Ribble with Langcliffe Mill over it on the right. After the next stile the walking becomes less muddy across the field diagonally to join the minor road at a gate by a sign.

Turn right, and after a couple of hundred yards, just before the trees on the left, some steps lead up to a gate stile, through which you pass. Turn right on the track which leads up above the trees, through a small wood, and at the footpath sign beyond the trees indicating Stainforth straight on, turn sharp left up the hill. At present this is not signed. You will see a scar, Reinsber Scar, in the distance: keep this well to your right, as the path is indistinct, leaving this field by a ladder stile, after which it becomes more obvious. It climbs a hill, and at the next wall take the left of two gaps (without gates), and carry on up the green track, which curves left, keeping a single hawthorn on your right. After a zig-zag the track turns right, on the level, till it meets a wall, where it turns left to round a right angle in the wall, then through a gate in the wall ahead.

Keep on this track, following roughly the wall on the right, with initially good views of Penyghent and Ingleborough, and near the field end pass through the wall via a gate, then quickly left through the next wall by another gate. The pasture is now delightfully limestone studded. At the next wall pass through a gate, carrying on the obvious track, curving to the left to go through a gate or over a ladder stile. Past this turn right up the hill by the wall, either direct or helped by a track coming over from the left, which turns right (east), to go through the wall you have followed up. This is all open access land.

Ahead you will see the entrance to Dead Man's Cave, a definite cave, but the forty foot passage for cavers is mostly a crawl. The route turns left and runs parallel to the wall on a green track. Over a rise the Celtic Wall appears to the right, with Smearsett Scar with its trig point beyond, and Penyghent to the right. Bear right to see this, then from its northwest end head in the direction of the wall till you meet a quad track, which winds its way down the bank, to pass through a fence at a gate, then go left over the wall by a ladder stile.

The Celtic Wall

This mysterious, isolated, and well preserved wall, measuring by my steps 22 yards long by five feet high and wide, is at SD 801674. It is not marked on the Ordnance Survey maps, which may partially explain why it is still there after what is thought to be over two thousand years. I hope this note doesn't alter that, although a dedicated walk to the wall by Wainwright has not done so. Wainwright thought it more likely to be a burial site rather than a defence for the encampment in the valley, an alternative proposition, although there is no evidence for its age, so I wonder am I promulgating a falsehood just because the master said so. Iron age burial habits were very diverse, but none that I could find involved a wall. If it had flags it would do for a prayer wall! The fact that it is a chain in length (10 chains = a furlong, 80 = a mile, 10x10 chains = 1 acre), a distance still used to measure railways and cricket pitches, for example, makes me wonder whether it is a bit more modern, as the chain was invented by the mathematical clergyman Edmund Gunter in 1620. There is a smaller fragment of wall in line with the main one, twice its length away, to the south east, which muddies things further.

Celtic Wall and Ingleborough

The path now leads to Feizor, although when you meet a wall and pass along its right side, make sure to cross it shortly by a ladder stile and follow its left side down. At the farm yard pass through a gate and either another one and short path to the café car park, or the farm track if unobstructed.

> **Pot Scar and Crummackdale**
> Two of Yorkshire's favourite climbing grounds, Pot Scar is the cliff you can see up to the right as you come to cross the wall before Feizor, and Crummackdale is the fine looking cliff you see up to the right when going up the lane from Wharfe later on. Pot Scar is not named on the maps, Crummackdale is named White Stone.

At the café, if not tempted by its delights, turn right up the metalled road through the charming hamlet of Feizor, and go over the hill, where the track loses the tarmac.

Feizor: from an Irish personal name Fiach, and norse Erg, a shieling ie a hut or summer cottage.

Looking ahead here to Moughton Scar (pronounced Moot'n) and Nab, note the upper rock, limestone, is horizontally layered, while the lower rock, Silurian grit/slate, is more vertical, a feature seen throughout Crummackdale. Just round the corner to the right the Dry Rigg Quarry has taken the hillside away for the gritstone to go on roads, but will not eat away what you see, they are only going deeper now. See Walk 9.

After a gate on the track go downhill, where after a couple of hundred yards go left over a ladder stile signed " Wharfe ¾". The path leads downhill via two gates and three ladder stiles to a minor road; turn right to cross a stream, then left over a stile, continuing north over two more ladder stiles unfortunately, with a bridge

Moughton Nab from Wharfe wood

over Wharfe Gill Syke in between. Over the last stile head obliquely left across the field to cross a clapper bridge, and yet another stile gets you onto the Austwick to Helwith Bridge Road. Turn left. There are now only three more stiles till Horton, honest!

After a hundred yards, as the road curves left, carry straight on up the private road to Wharfe, a delightful hamlet. The road curves round left and becomes a bridleway, which continues above the main hamlet to join an enclosed lane heading northwest. This leads uphill past two barns on the left, and at the top, as it curves to the left, go over the stile on the right or use the gate just beyond it. Follow the field path in the same direction as the lane, through a gap in the first wall, then head for the "pass" or col straight ahead, as the lane bears away to the left. Go through this pass, and as you see the next wall ahead, curve round right to go up alongside a stream eastwards. You will

Path through Wharfe

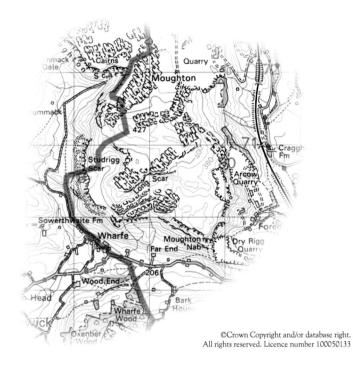

Penyghent from Moughton summit

see an inset cliff, actually a dry waterfall, where the scar (Studrigg) dips. Head for this. The path crosses the stream and heads for the scree, passing right, up between banks of scree then zig-zagging up to pass over a ladder stile about a hundred yards left of the dip.

> **Crummackdale unconformity**
> You will have noticed the horizontal strata of limestone
> above the vertical plates of Silurian rock on Moughton
> Scar as you came over the hill from Feizor. This feature
> occurs elsewhere in Crummackdale, particularly on
> Studrigg Scar further north than our route up it,
> SD781709, where there is no obscuring scree. It is seen
> best from below so you could walk north (rough and
> difficult to get close), and then return to the route. The
> unconformity here means that the horizontal limestone is
> immediately above the off-vertical Silurian grit, whereas
> in geological time there should be a layer between, about
> 50 million years worth of layer!

To get to the top of Moughton, head half left from the ladder
stile towards the hill, easier to take the right fork in the path
before it curves round to the right, and gently ascend leftwards
into a raised amphitheatre SD 784710. Cross this and climb
the far bank, and soon you will spy the trig point marking the
summit. There are a variety of small paths. The panorama is
superb: Penyghent ahead eastwards, the Ribblehead moors
northward, then continuing anti-clockwise, Ingleborough, the
Lune valley with the Bowland Fells beyond, and Pendle Hill
southwards.

Now aim west of north down towards the obvious area of
limestone pavement, through juniper and heather, an uncommon
pair for limestone terrain. Tracts of grass help your progress. Some
shooting butts are passed on the way to a low gully leading through
the pavements westwards, which you can take for easier walking.
Otherwise traverse the pavement, heading for the right end of
the obvious Moughton Scars in the distance. The grykes (gaps)
between the clints (rocks), harbour flowers and ferns, especially
the distinctive hart's tongue fern, where sheep cannot easily feed.

If the gully is taken, at the end of the pavement area turn northwards on a good path to join the large one coming up from Crummackdale past a memorial cairn. Carry on slightly rightwards, on a cairned path between fairly decrepit grouse shooting butts. At the next wall a sign on this side indicates Horton left, but go over the ladder stile to turn left beside the wall in a part of Ingleborough National Nature Reserve.

Ingleborough National Nature Reserve

An area of 1,014 hectares mainly north and east of the summit, created by the European Union as part of a "Natura 2000" series between 2004 and 2006. (A hectare is a metric unit, and as the chain was explained above, I'd better explain that a hectare is 100x100 square metres, one hectare being 2.47 acres!) It is a site of special scientific interest (SSSI) and a special area of conservation (SAC) managed by Natural England. One of the worthy aims of this particular reserve, it seems to me, would be to prevent Horton quarry gobbling up more of Moughton. For more about the Reserve, see Walk 9.

At the next wall a gate leads out of the reserve, the path turning half right across the moor to a large signpost, where follow the large path rightwards winding down to Horton. This, of course, is the incredibly busy Three Peaks route, marked by cairns and low wooden posts with yellow rings, presumably to aid night travel.

The station is thankfully after the last field, and you have to cross the line, carefully, if travelling back to Settle.

5. SETTLE TO RIBBLEHEAD VIA NORBER AND INGLEBOROUGH

Start: Settle Station
Finish: Ribblehead Station
14.5 miles.   2,930 ft. ascent.   8 hours.
Summits: Ingleborough, 2372ft., 723m., (M,H).

A long, lovely, straightforward walk via Feizor (café), strange Norber Scar and its erratic boulders, Ingleborough and its northeast ridge, which is unashamedly the first day of my "Settle to Carlisle" eight day walk, with a different ending to avoid the road walk and see the remains of a Viking settlement.

If you haven't eaten breakfast before this walk, then the Feizor Café, some two and a half miles on does a splendid one, and is open from 9.30am seven days a week at the time of writing.

Go down to Station Road and turn left under the railway. About 150 yards past the turning on the right after the school a signed footpath goes right, past the back of the school and conveniently (if you need provisions) right onto the front of Booths' supermarket. The path continues in the same line beyond Booths' carpark to join a road. Turn left and just after the fire station turn left onto the footpath/cycleway. This leads to a lane, leading round right, and past Kings Mill flats. Past this you see the river Ribble on the left, cross this by the bridge and turn right on the RW, leading pleasantly past Settle College, a 13 to 19 comprehensive, to cross the main road.

Carry on here on the enclosed path between playing fields, and after a short dogleg and a gated stile, the next field is crossed on an obvious open path. Two more stiles and you are on a wooded bank above the Ribble with Langcliffe Mill over it on the right. After the next stile the walking becomes less muddy across the field diagonally to join the minor road at a gate by a sign.

Turn right, and after a couple of hundred yards, just before the trees on the left, some steps lead up to a gate stile, through which you pass. Turn right on the track which leads up above the trees, through a small wood, and at the footpath sign beyond the trees

Near Feizor

Pot Scar from Feizor

Spring flowers in Oxenber Wood

indicating Stainforth straight on, turn sharp left up the hill. At present this is not signed. You will see a scar, Reinsber Scar, in the distance; keep this well to your right, as the path is indistinct, leaving this field by a ladder stile, where it becomes more obvious. It climbs a hill, and at the next wall take the left of two gaps (without gates), and carry on up the green track, which curves left, keeping a single hawthorn on your right. After a zig-zag the track turns right, on the level, till it meets a wall, where it turns left to round a right angle in the wall, then goes through a gate in the wall ahead. Keep on this track, following roughly the wall on the right, with initially good views of Penyghent and Ingleborough. Near the field end pass through the wall via a gate, then quickly left through the next wall by another gate.

The pasture is now delightfully limestone studded. At the next wall pass through a gate, carrying on along the obvious track, which curves to the left to go through a gate or over a ladder stile. You are now free of further obstructions and you can sail down to Feizor, where a farmhouse café mentioned above is open every day.

As you approach Feizor, you will see an impressive limestone cliff to the right, Pot Scar, a popular climbing venue, hence its' somewhat polished rock.

As you join the minor road in Feizor, turn right for the café, which is then on your left.

Feeling refreshed, continue westwards on a path just down from the café, signed Austwick, which leads through fields with Oxenber Wood on the right. You will see an entry point to the wood as the path passes near it, with an explanatory board.

If an extra 200 feet of climbing and a few hundred yards don't put you off, enter the wood (SD 780680) and go up through the flowers on a walk with red marked posts as a guide. This forks left at a clearing on top, and descends to join a path where turn left and soon join Wood Lane and our route.

> **Oxenber Wood**
> The wood is part of Old Woodland Restoration, a project managed by English Nature, and in spring it is literally carpeted with woodland flowers. In late April the display is predominantly primroses and wood anemones, the bluebells coming on later, ie in May, but in a late spring all of these can magically appear together, plus early purple orchids. From midsummer on though, the flowers are disappointing.

If not tempted by the wood, carry on along the Austwick path and where it hits a track, turn right and pass Wood House on the track, carrying straight on or actually half left at the junction with Wood Lane, to cross Austwick beck on Flascoe Bridge and join the B road from Austwick. Turn left towards the village and after about 150 yards turn right up Townhead Lane.

You will note I have skilfully avoided Austwick, where the devil lurks in the form of a decent pub at lunchtime, the Gamecock. An excellent picnic spot exists among the Norber erratics, if you can last till then.

> **Norber erratics**
> Erratics are lumps of rock which shouldn't be where they are, because they were transported by a glacier in the last Ice Age, in this case from half a mile up the valley. They are Silurian slate/grit, dark grey, and rest on carboniferous limestone, an obvious contrast. Geologically the limestone was laid down on the slate. The main boulder field is above Nappa Scars, and a weird and wonderful sight it is. The softer limestone has eroded around the bases, except where sheltered directly underneath, so they are suspended on their pedestals. Some boulders may rock on the pedestals when, inevitably, you will wish to be photographed on top of one, so be careful you may be the first to topple one!
>
> Actually, although this is of no use at all to you on this walk, the best place to view the phenomenon is from higher up and in the evening light, with shadows cast by each boulder. Then you can see that there are more down below in the first field you cross after leaving the road, except here the bases have been buried by accumulation of soil over centuries.

Carry on up Townhead Lane, until a couple of hundred yards beyond the last houses where the road is crossed by the track of Thwaite Lane. Turn left here and after about fifty yards turn right, heading up the field and eventually following the wall on its left side. Note the half buried erratics as mentioned above. Note also on your left skyline the fine outline of Robin Proctor Scar, now full of hard bolted climbs, whereas more traditional Yorkshire limestone climbs are eastwards across the valley on Crummackdale, marked White Stone on the 1:25,000 map.

At the top of this first field on the left side cross a stile, the gate having been locked for years, and go up past a small cliff on your right. You can now wander upwards to find and traverse the erratic field at will, but I recommend the following route for maximum effect: follow the path round

Approaching Norber erratics

right, parallel to the wall, up some natural limestone steps, then, opposite a stile in the wall, turn left on a narrow path. You are now in the erratic field, and eventually you will find a broad green path leading upwards. Leave this obliquely right when you see a high ladder stile in the top right hand side of this field, on another narrow path.

Over the ladder stile you are on the open fell. You can find your own way to the crest of the fell, which is cairned, but for easier progress underfoot and to avoid too much limestone pavement, find the path twenty yards up from the stile, turn right on it and on the next brow you will see a notch on the skyline about half a mile away. Head for this via whichever path suits you, travelling diagonally upwards. The notch is a narrow defile from which the stones have been removed to form a sort of wall on the right side, which makes for easy progress. Through this a thin path goes down into a wide bowl and along the base of a shoulder on your left, then up and eventually joins the wide path from Clapham to Selside.

The aim now is to locate a path which cuts the corner up to Ingleborough, heading for Nick Pot. First find the junction of paths marked by a PBW post, SD 767720. Your path leaves the wide green track to Sulber Gate leftwards, 200 yards past this junction, just after a small cairn to the right of the track. The "shortcut" wends its way between the bare limestone and joins the main path up from Horton near Nick Pot, an obvious pothole.

The path is now a main thoroughfare and you will not be alone. The next wall coming down from Simon Fell is crossed by a stile, then the broad stony path leads gradually upwards until the final steepening, which is now mostly stepped, leading onto the plateau. The summit is further on with a trig point, cairn and cruciate walled shelter.

Ingleborough Hill Fort?

It used to be thought that the summit was a fortified Iron Age village, as there was evidence of "huts" and "ramparts". Hence its name: burh in Old English is fortified place. Very recent expert opinion, as outlined by a notice on the Clapham path, puts the earthworks in the Bronze Age. The circular remains are thought to be ring cairns, and the purpose for ritual, not as a fort. Makes more sense.

You will have noticed a change in vegetation and rock around the wall coming south from Simon Fell, limestone giving way to shale and sandstone, with the summit plinth of millstone grit.

Ingleborough and the north ridge from Gearstones

The route to Ribblehead retraces its steps, literally, off the summit but keeps on in the same east-north-east direction when meeting the path up from Horton on which you arrived. This descends further, and when the main path to Chapelle-Dale descends north, keep going round the great curved rim of Simon Fell on a good path, descending the north ridge of Simon Fell to a broad col, then slightly

ascending Park Fell. On meeting a wall on the far side of Park Fell, turn left, still on a definite path, and descend towards Colt Park. After a little wooden gate, head for the wall descending on your left. Go over this wall via a step-stile by a post, as the ground levels out, or by a gate a bit lower down. Carry on northwards on a variety of

Ingleborough from the ridge

paths to go through the gate in the wall about 150 yards west of the wall you've accompanied down. The last bit is over limestone pavement. Follow the short green marked posts back to the gate into Gauber Quarry with a yellow danger sign on it, or, if you haven't yet seen the Viking settlement, follow the instructions as for Walk 11.

Marker posts take you through Gauber Quarry, which nature has not quite naturally recolonised yet, and onto the track to Ribblehead. Unfortunately there is no direct route to the station, you have to pass the Station Inn for a drink then double back!

While waiting for the train south, look at the northbound platform and wonder that from 1975 to 1993 it did not exist, having been taken out by BR to make new sidings for their ballast quarry.

6. BOWLAND CIRCULAR VIA GISBURN FOREST, KNOTTERANUM AND BOWLAND KNOTTS

Start and Finish: Settle Station.
15.1 miles.   1897 ft., ascent.   7½ Hrs.
Summits: Bowland Knotts, 1404 ft., 428m.
Google Earth: Possibly helpful for Coney Garth pillow mounds, see text.

A long walk, the third longest, and the roughest and boggiest, on the "dark", gritstone side of Settle. For those tiring of lovely Yorkshire limestone or Cumbria grandeur, as it sneaks into Lancashire. A pleasant introduction, then a short very rough passage through Gisburn Forest, more boggy moorland to a Bowland high road pass, open views on the return and interest in Giggleswick with the school and chapel. This will not become a classic walk, more of a cult one: do not do it as a first walk from this book. The only walk where gaiters are recommended if at all wet.

Down from the station turn left to pass under the line, left again and follow the main road round to the right and over the Ribble at Penny Bridge. Just before the first house on the left a gate leads to the RW path, the sign for which is on the right side of the road.

The path leads to the river to follow it downstream. As the telegraph line joins you and you cross a small beck, turn right after the gate and follow the hedge then wall up to

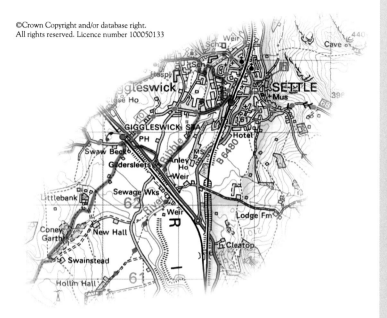

Gildersleets. Through two gates, take the short track to the old road, right to the new one, right on this. A hundred yards up turn left up a "dead end" lane, alongside Swaw beck.

This leads onto the Settle by-pass, which you must cross to continue on the path by the beck, and up to the B road from Settle. Turn left here under the Leeds to Lancaster railway and immediately left over a stile "Public footpath Littlebank". Follow the wall on the left round to a gate or stile at the top. Head for a stile straight ahead, then a hundred yards down go over a gap stile in the wall on your right, before the barn. Follow the wall on your left to Littlebank Barn, through a gap stile in the corner at the bottom. Pass through a short field to a gate, then briefly into the farmyard on the right, then left through the gates heading for the stile in the wall to the right of the bungalow.

Head across the next field to the left of the barn underneath "Lumb", to pass through a stile just past a tiny stream. Yellow markers appear here, follow them, not, as indicated on the map, into the trees across a bog, but on a newly diverted path to the left of the bog to the next yellow marked post, then through a metal gate plus post. Go up the bank to cross the track to another Littlebank, and carry on up the bank left, to a marker post between two trees. Carry on more or less level, aiming to the right of a pallet you can see in the next fence, to cross it by a wooden stile.

Climb the bank to your right gently, as you must cross the wall on the right as it descends, by a gated step-stile. Traverse left above the wood till it ends, then go through a wooden gate.

> **Coney Garth**
> The hill you have passed under, Coney Garth, means "fenced area of rabbits", which fits with the caption of Pillow Mounds on the map. See Walk 21 for a description of pillow mounds. However, I could see no evidence of such mounds on the ground, just the possibility of two higher on the hill on Google Earth. Perhaps they are hidden in the trees.

Cross the stream and turn left on a raised embankment, then right at the track of Swainstead Raike, which takes you to a minor road from Rathmell. Strictly speaking a path should be taken left off the track, but it leads through a bog so I should keep on it if I were you.

At the road turn right, which has some decent flora on its verges, past Lower Sheep Wash, and as the road swings north take the track straight on to Upper Sheep Wash. The footpath turns right just before a cattle grid to go over Rathmell Beck by a small bridge and then rejoins the track, although this seems rather pointless. Through the farmyard

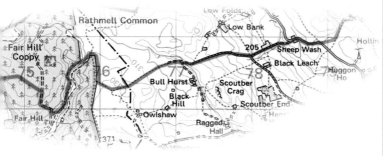

and up the lane, turn half right as a track comes in from the left. There is a gate as the open access land is entered, when the track curves right, then becomes a green track following the wall on the left, then a path. Over a gap stile carry on through a bog with reedgrass to carry on beside the next wall heading west. The next wall has a gap to pass through, and no footbridge to cross the stream.

You are now in Lancashire. Carry on up the slope aiming to the right of a sycamore tree to pass through a gap stile in the wall. Note Whelpstone Crag to the left: going to the crag and then through the forest is no improvement on the route so forget it!

Head half right, through gaps in the short wall on top of the hill and head to the forest boundary. The path going north is between the wall and the forest fence, and although it is all boggy, it is pleasanter to stay outside the wall.

Gisburn Forest and moors

Gisburn Forest

An extensive plantation managed by Forest Enterprise, who have opened it up for public usage, especially for mountain bikers. Purpose built trails have been built for their use. Walking trails are nearer the southern end, but the management do not discourage access anywhere or exits from the boundaries as long as there is no forestry work going on, and you do not damage the boundary fences/walls. There has been extensive cutting down of the conifers and replanting with broadleaved species, but it will take twenty years or more to mature. Prior to 1974 it was all in Yorkshire, the West Riding.

At the forest corner two wooden stiles cross the fences to allow you to turn down left along the forest edge, crossing a bog to follow a grassy bank. At the stream cross the wire fence on your left by a hidden stile near the stream, easily cross the stream, and continue down the valley. There is no path. The next half mile is awful: stumps of conifers, forest debris, bogs, and other obstacles abound. Cross the stream to suit. It gets better, specifically at

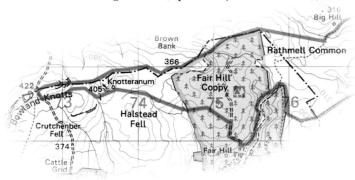

a forest track which you gain by ascending the bank of cut conifers on the right when you can see the ruins of Dob Dale on the east bank.

Turn right up the track, through the spruces and foxgloves, turning left then right, and about 120 yards after the right turn, at SD 752602, take the forest break going half left. There is one opposite going half right. At the time of writing small red flags indicate all of the way to the forest boundary; leave the forest break in a small depression where it meets a ruined wall, and head left down the line of another ruined wall (red flags) to exit the forest by a short length of wire fence easily crossed at SD 747604.

Turn right up the moor and then left to follow the rough line of Brock Clough Beck. The going is pathless but not too rough, and you can look for cranberries which grow here. Head for the wooden shooting hut as it appears, under the eastern end of the Knotteranum.

The going is better on top of the ridge, the jumble of gritstone rocks being mostly at the southern edge. The wall separating Knotteranum and Bowland Knotts has a stile about sixty yards from the east-west ridge wall, and a gate further south. It's better walking near the top wall. The only short cliff of this ridge is facing west at Bowland Knotts; admire this and head over the cattle grid on the road to turn east for home on a definite path, sometimes a boggy quad track, which takes an undulating course to the Resting Stone by the northeast edge of Gisburn Forest.

Knotteranum

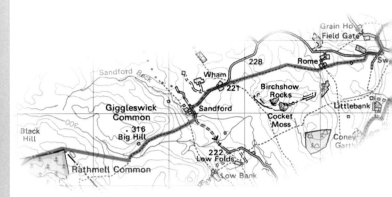

The wind is now behind you, the sun on your right, and Settle in the distance with the Three Peaks beyond, and you are back in Yorkshire since the cattle grid. The going may be boggy in places but is better than this morning.

From the Resting Stone cross the moor on a bearing just south of east, skirting the obvious boggy sections, to pick up the path leading towards Sandford Farm. This is definite beyond the stream crossing, but not before it. The path skirts below Big Hill, passes some shooting butts and a ruin on the left, and roughly sticks to the boundary between the bracken and the moor. The atrocity of Giggleswick Quarry is evident ahead, with the sharp edge of Fountains Fell to the right, then, further right you're looking up the Stockdale valley with Rye Loaf Hill on its right.

At the minor road from Rathmell turn left, follow it round right, noting the wall on the right has flat sandstone/grit flags on top, not the usual half upright ones. At the corner below Lower Wham, go through the gate on the right and up a track through another gate. Ahead are Birchshow Rocks, but the path goes left to follow the wall past some unnamed rocks on the next hill, with good bouldering here, but they are on private ground.

After the third gap stile since the road the wall ends; go half right across the next field to an obvious further gap stile, then head to the right of Farther Rome, the rightmost of the two buildings which come into view, as this line skirts a large depression on the way to the next gap stile in the wall. Go left through a metal gate, then right through some boggy land to the right corner of the house, through a metal gate and turn right, past the front of the house and through a gate on the left, to head east. Another gate is passed then the path leads down to cross a fence by a wooden stile, and up to a gate by the barn at the top. Aim to the right of the trees; a thin gap stile leads to a small field, turn left and another gap stile leads to a minor road.

Turn down right. At the B road junction you can give up

Giggleswick School and Chapel

and take the road right all the way back, or rather back to where you joined it this morning, and reverse that bit, or come with me to Giggleswick for a bit more interest.

Turn left up the B road, right at the first corner through a gate "Public Footpath", and head obliquely down left to the bottom corner, where a gap stile leads to a bridge, then a lane leading under the railway and bypass, into Close House. Through a gate go half left on a metalled road, till you meet a public footpath post with three directions. Take the half right one up a track, soon spying the dome of the Giggleswick School Chapel. Just after the second barn on the right go over the fence on the right by a wooden stile towards the dome. A gate leads to a lane, turn right, but where the left enclosing wall bears left from the track, follow it leftwards aiming for a gate to the left of the Chapel. Through this a green lane leads north to a road past the private Chapel, where turn right and admire the school buildings.

Giggleswick School and Chapel

This is a co-educational private school, part boarding, part day, celebrating 500 years of use in 2012. The land belonged to the ancient church of St. Alkelda, owned by the Prior of Durham, who leased the land for the school. The Chapel was donated by Walter Morrison of Malham for Queen Victoria's Diamond Jubilee. It was finished in 1901. It is part built on naked gritstone, the walls merging with the stone, and the presence of the copper dome was a condition of the donor, who wanted an eastern, Palestinian theme. More details, many more, from the school's website. The Chapel is open Mon. to Frid. 9-5, but you have to get the key from Main School reception.

Carry on down through Giggleswick, alongside a delightful stream briefly, past the village church and the Black Horse pub. You might want to stop here for a drink or two, there are no more pubs the way I'm taking you.

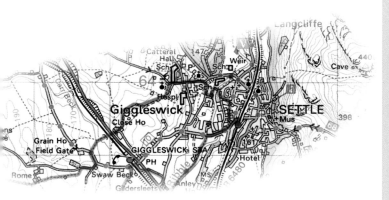

At the T junction keep on right down Bankwell Road, till just past a house with a red door, where turn left down a ginnel "public footpath", to come out at the Ribble and cross the bridge here.

Keep following the road round Kings Mill flats until you see a blue cycle/footpath sign a hundred yards up on the left. Follow this to the road by the fire station, turn first right to pass in front of Booths. Carry on past a primary school, and turn left at the road for the station.

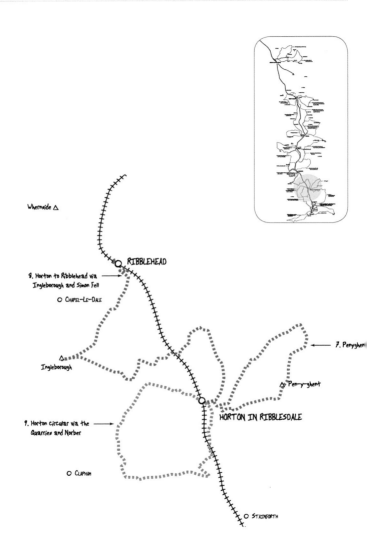

Whernside △

○ RIBBLEHEAD

8. Horton to Ribblehead via
Inglbeborough and Simon Fell

○ CHAPEL-LE-DALE

△ Inglborough

7. Penyghent

△ Pen-y-ghent

HORTON IN RIBBLESDALE

9. Horton circular via the
Quarries and Norber

○ CLAPHAM

○ STAINFORTH

7. PENYGHENT

Start and Finish: Horton-in-Ribblesdale Station

8.9 miles.   1913 ft. ascent.   4 hours.
Summits: Penyghent, 2277 ft., 694m., (M,H); Plover
Hill, 2231 ft., 680m., (H).
Google Earth: Of no special use.

Mostly easy walking, but with a short steep section which is a little scrambly. Excellent views. A moorland ridge away from the crowds leads down to a good track back via a large "pothole". Good for a lazy summer's day. It can be shortened to go with the crowds.

Go down the station road in Horton-in-Ribblesdale to the main road and on to cross the Ribble by the footbridge just before the Crown. (Toilets in the car park here.) Exit the car park south on the road, and turn left up a track a hundred yards after the famous café. Signed "Public Bridleway and the Pennine Way, Foxup Lane". Just past the last house on the right go over a stile and up and over the hill, to come out on a lane by an unmarked gap stile midway between gates at either end of the wall. Or avoid the stiles by keeping up the lane and turning right after passing through a gate.

Go down the lane to a side road and over the Douks Gill or Ghyll as the OS shows it,

Penyghent from Horton-in-Ribblesdale

by the bridge ahead. Turn up the lane through a delightful wooded area, with many wild flowers to note. At the barn of Brackenbottom, turn left through a gate signed "Penyghent Summit 1¾ ml", then a small gate to follow the wall on its right side up the hill.

A couple of small limestone scars are passed easily. Near the top parts of the path have been constructed, some with flagstones. Cast your eye to the summit crag, which is of gritstone, above the shorter limestone crags.

Climbing on Penyghent.

Several climbs on excellent gritstone exist on the west facing summit crag, including one in "Classic Rock", Red Pencil, so called as a red pencil was found there by the first ascenscionist. I was told off here by the gamekeeper in the early 1990s, shooting foxes, he said, it was private land, he said. He had a gun, so although he calmed down quite a bit, we left! Now on open access land, of course, but recent rockfall means caution is urged.

At the top wall go through a gate and left on the PW, the path now mainly constructed for that highway, to pass through a small limestone scar by worn rock steps, then onto gritstone terrain, with a small step higher up passed on either side. The summit trig point is an easy walk away now, go left there over a small gated gap stile and enjoy the view.

Penyghent from ascent path

Penyghent

I prefer Wainwright's spelling as you can see. The name means hill/head (pen), of the border/winds (ghent), take your pick. The geology is very much in layers as outlined in the Geology section: you have come up on Great Scar Limestone till just before the PW, then onto Yoredale Series, the limestone part of which you scrambled through, then the gritstone took over, and continues until you descend through the Yoredale limestone band, then sandstone moors coming off Plover Hill.

The view from the summit is superb: Ingleborough dominates to the west, with Pendle Hill in Lancashire way off to the south of it; rightwards from Ingleborough the Lake District Fells can be seen far away before the nearer gentle curve of Whernside; then the Howgills, Baugh Fell, the long ridge of Wild Boar Fell with its clear sharp flank, seen over Great Knoutberry Hill and nearer still Cam Fell ridge with its plantation; due north is Great Shunner Fell, then round to the east the Swaledale and Wharfedale hills.

Purple Saxifrage.
Saxifraga oppostifolia, an arctic flower left over from the last Ice Age, is found on the sunny limestone slopes of Penyghent from mid March to mid April. Classically found just off the main western descent route near the limestone pinnacle, it is also found just off the ascent route by the limestone scar. Worth looking at a Youtube video by David and Audrey Crossley to see where.

Follow the path alongside the wall on the gritstone moorland to Plover Hill, mildly boggy after the turn to

Penyghent from the west

the east. Cloudberry leaves abound here in summer, the flowers are shier. Over the ladder stile on the summit plateau, the summit is 100 yards further on. The wide path off goes north to a marker post and descends to the wall where recent steps have eased the passage down through the limestone cliffs, but mucked about with the flowers here, including mossy saxifrage (which you will see in abundance in Horton Scar Lane).

Penyghent south, gritstone band and cliffs

At the Foxup path, turn left for home, Ingleborough always in view, with the flank of our hill gradually revealing more of itself.

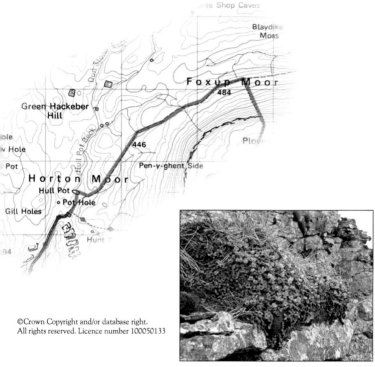

Purple Saxifrage on the eastern cliffs

The first path crossing is the constructed one for the Three Peaks Route (pity the poor souls at this stage of their "challenge"), then the path winds down to go along and through the wall by a gate in front of the huge gash of Hull Pot, worth a visit.

Pennine Way descent from Penhyghent

> **Hull Pot**
> 300 feet long and 60 feet wide and deep, this gash has a dry waterfall on its north wall, but when wet the beck pours over and indeed the whole pot has been known to fill up. Not good then for any cavers caught in the system entered by the caves at the east end. The water "resurgence" is at Brants Gill Head, west of Horton Scar Lane, as it is normally for all water sinking on Penyghent and Fountains Fell, but in floods it resurges at Douk Ghyll Cave and becomes the stream you crossed earlier in Horton.

Continue south to join the PW coming down from the hill. Through a gate it is Horton Scar Lane, relieved lower down by masses of varied flowers on the sides. Back at the road the Crown and its extensive beer garden awaits you before the station.

Pinnacle near descent on Pennine Way

Hull Pot

8. HORTON TO RIBBLEHEAD VIA INGLEBOROUGH AND SIMON FELL

Start: Horton-in-Ribblesdale Station.
Finish: Ribblehead Station.
12.2 miles. 2381 ft., ascent. 2161 ft., descent.
5½ hours.
Summits: Ingleborough, 2372 ft., 723 m., (M,H);
Simon Fell, 2133 ft., 650 m.,(H).

The easy introduction up the Pennine, Ribble, and Pennine bridleways allows at least half of the well-used highway from Horton up Ingleborough to be avoided, and the natural sanctuary of South House Pavement to be visited. Just one locked gate and five yards of private land prevent a completely different ascent via Borrins Moor, one the cyclo-cross event uses. Ah well.

Go down to the B6479 and straight along it to the Crown, to start up the combined PW and RW track at the far end of the carpark. This climbs gently to give views over Ribblesdale, with your hills of this afternoon over leftwards, Ingleborough largely hidden by the mass of Simon Fell. The first point of interest is Sell Gill Holes.

Sell Gill Holes

Sell Gill Holes

You can clearly see the two entrances on either side of the track here; the "normal" entrance is to the left down a dry gully, and is dry, but don't go too near, as a fall into it would, at best require a ladder rescue, at worst a coffin. The "wet route" on the right is where the stream sinks into a slit. This might be worth exploring if the rocks were utterly dry.

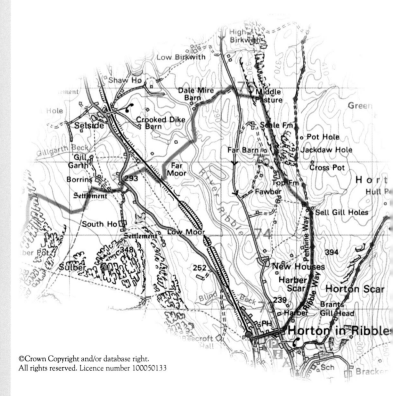

Fifty yards past the next gate branch left by a sign "FP Birkwith 1 7/8 ", then cross a ladder stile with a RW sign by it, an R with a squashed W under it, by the second ruined building. Just past the ruin turn right through a metal gate, and head to the ladder stile at the end of the next field, then another. The wide path now goes unhindered till a stile opposite Scale Farm. After the next gate turn left off the RW over a ladder stile marked "Footpath". Go obliquely down rightwards and when you see the lower wall of the field, head for a wooden gate in it where a fence meets the wall. Turn right up the road, and after a couple of hundred yards turn left onto the marked PBW. This is a tractor track to Dale Mire Barn, but after the left turn is a newly constructed path, crossing the Ribble by a splendid new three arch wooden bridge. It was here, on the 12th June 2012, that the PBW was finally opened, by Martin Clunes. The access under the Railway was not secured until a month or so before the opening!

As the bridleway joins the main road I prefer to cross it without deviating left, and go through the stile to "South House", walking on turf to join the bridleway again on the left. Make sure to turn right here and not end up at South House. The "Settlement" marked on the map on the right is frankly disappointing, just a few grass embankments.

Over a ford and through two gates the track enters the Ingleborough National Nature Reserve, which is open access. Continue southwards, watching for the first gate in the wall on the right, to

The PBW Ribble bridge

pass through this or a step-stile. A quad track leads up and rightwards, then left by a water trough to the top wall. Here, pass through a small gate to a long, thin, enclosure, South House Pavement. A ladder stile a hundred yards opposite the gate leads out of this little haven.

> **South House Pavement**
> Part of the Ingleborough National Nature Reserve, it was leased to them in 1975 since when it has been allowed to develop naturally, ie sheep excluded, but also with some "weeding" of bracken and rosebay willowherb, for example. It is mainly pavement of the Great Scar Limestone, with tall flowers such as meadowsweet, spear thistle and blue moor grass growing out of the grykes, and limestone ferns, hairy stonecrop, bedstraw and narrow leaved bittercress (buttercress in the internet info!) between them. Early spring sees primroses, coltsfoots, wood anemones and dog's mercury aplenty. Trees are mainly north of your passage through.

There are only two ways past the walls of the large enclosure of Fell Close: a gate at the northeast corner, which unfortunately leads onto private land where a locked gate could give access to Borrins Moor. This is the route of the Three Peaks cyclo-cross event, accessing Simon's Fell near the top by a wide stile named Rawnsley's Leap, after John Rawnsley, the current organiser and original winner in of that event 1961. Special permission is granted for the event to pass through the private land, which you have not got, and so unfortunately, I cannot advise the route.

The second exit is via a wooden step-stile at the south-eastern corner, to the main path from Horton. To get there walk along the top side of the impressive pavement and then turn left at the end.

Sulber Pot
A short detour to the west just before the wall by the main path brings the 27 by 14 foot gash of Sulber Pot into view. The chamber below is roughly twice the size of the gash. A metal ladder down at least 50 feet might tempt an exploration, but the top is held by an old rope at present and I would not descend unless someone reliable is at the top!

On the main path turn right immediately through a gate and follow the highway to the top of Ingleborough as for Walk 5. On returning from the summit plateau down Swine Tail, carry on in the line of the Tail when the path you came up branches right, and when you reach the wall coming from Simon Fell pass through the gate. Rather than contouring along the western edge of the long ridge as for Walk 5, follow the

Simon Fell and Moughton Scars from Moughton

wall on its left side to Simon Fell. The "summit" is somewhat disappointing. Cross a stile beside a locked wooden gate just after the fell top and carry on along the ridge on the right side of the wall now.

Park Fell is at least marked by a trig point, the path deviating from the wall as it climbs the fell, and at the crossroads by a small tarn turn left for the summit. After this pass through a gate on the right at the corner, then over a stile back left, to follow the fence down the steep end of the fell. After a little wooden gate, head for the wall descending on your left. Go over this wall via a step-stile by a post, as the ground levels

out, or by a gate a bit lower down. Carry on northwards on a variety of paths to go through the gate in the wall about a hundred and fifty yards west of the wall you've accompanied down. The last bit is over limestone pavement. Follow the short green marked posts back to the gate into Gauber Quarry with a yellow danger sign on it, or if you haven't yet seen the Viking settlement, follow the instructions as for Walk 11.

There is no legal way direct from the quarry road to the station, so unfortunately you'll have to pass the Inn again and take refreshments.

Viking remains, Gauber

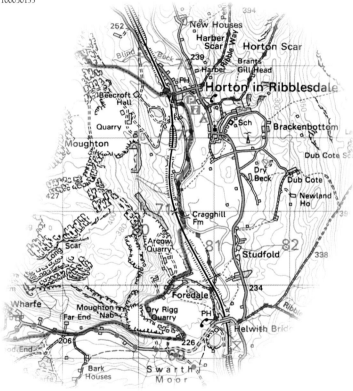

9. HORTON CIRCULAR VIA THE QUARRIES AND NORBER

Start and finish: Horton-in Ribblesdale Station.
9.8 miles.   1305 ft., ascent.   4½ hours.
Summits: none
Google Earth: of no special use.

An interesting mixture of the modern man-made, the three quarries, and the ancient natural, the Norber erratics, on generally easy terrain. There are no toilets at Horton station. If needed, the facilities in the village car park are accessed by heading towards the Ribble by the main road and going over the footbridge on the right.

From the station descend the road, turning right onto Cragg Hill Road just before the main road. A short way along this turn left along a track, signed "Poppy Cottage" and turn right at the bottom to meet the RW coming over a stile from the left, to join the Ribble side.

If the toilets were visited, return over the footbridge and go through a gap in the road wall to follow the Ribbleside path to reach the same point.

The path descends some steps and goes along a concrete embankment, which would be tricky in spate, the field being then a better option. Carry on the obvious path through the fields by the river to Cragghill Farm. Keep on past the metal Ribble footbridge for seventy yards on the farm track, then go right over an (as yet) unmarked wooden stile beyond some boggy ground, into a scruffy farmyard with bales and disused machines. Go straight across this for twenty yards to an unmarked gate, then straight up again to an obvious railway gate. I have checked this route, indeed had to find it out from the farmer, who suggested I contact the "Park Authority" to get some signs. There should be some eventually.

Over the railway a sign to Foredale indicates left. Head towards the mid point of the far wall of the field at a dogleg, where a stile leads to a field with a thin path leading gently up to a gated stile, "FP Foredale 5/8" You're now on the side of Arcow Quarry, although you can't see it. An annoying ladder stile takes you back to the lower left side of the wall, where a very good made path on the bank up from the flood plain takes you over three wall stiles and onto a track turning right, through a gate and then joins the main quarry road. Interestingly the wall you have followed does not appear to be of quarried gritstone, but of limestone. Soon turn left into Foredale farm, the right branch going into Arcow Quarry.

Arcow Quarry

This quarry, owned by Tarmac, does not advertise its wares on the internet. It calls itself Arcow Slate Quarry, but the "slate", is gritstone as for Dry Rigg Quarry, (see later), used for road resurfacing. The Yorkshire Dales National Park Authority (YDNPA) has granted quarrying rights till June 2015, allowing the movement of 240-300,000 tonnes of rock per year, or 220 lorry loads. Compare this with Dry Rigg, 300-330,000 tonnes, 250 lorry loads, to assess the relative sizes, although see "Dry Rigg Quarry" for the latest restrictions on that figure. There are twelve (local) employees, and sixteen for Dry Rigg, which leads into the local argument between the "green conservationist" (ecofascist to the other side), and the local "good for the district" factions.

As the road curves severely right and up to the row of houses above, carry straight on through a gate marked with a white rectangle on its post. The road used to give access to the disused Foredale Quarry, for a short time used by climbers, but now the sign is specific in not allowing vehicles/walkers.

Quarries from near Jubilee cave

At the quarry sign you are diverted left onto the Newfield Bridleway, and a short way along it is worth turning up right to the viewing area for Dry Rigg Quarry. On your return note the area to the north is a raised peat bog, Swarth moor, an SSSI, managed by Natural England and monitored by Lafarge.

Dry Rigg Quarry

This large quarry is the most outgoing of the three by far, having an extensive website and two special viewing areas. It advertises itself as only one of six in the country producing high quality stone for highway surfacing, high quality meaning skid and wear resistant. Arcow is obviously another, Ingleton a third in the National Park. The rock is gritstone from the Silurian period. It is owned by Lafarge, head office in Paris, and on the day we did the walk the news came out that they had won a case with the YDNPA to continue operations till late 2021, on the condition that they must sign an undertaking to limit their road haulage to effectively half of the present amount by the end of 2013. This is obviously a nudge to obtain a rail connection to the Settle to Carlisle line. There are sixteen local employees, see "Arcow Quarry".

Dry Rigg Quarry

Going east allows an excellent view of Penyghent. The bridleway then curves round the quarry and turns west, joining the tarmac access road for a short while. As the road curves left to the main road, carry straight on to a footpath signed "Newfield ¾". The wide path curves round right by the quarry wall past a small quarry mere on the right, then climbs a hill into a corridor between two walls. The quarry wall on the right is made of gritstone from the quarry, some of the stones being faced with calcite, the most stable polymorph of calcium carbonate. Calcite will dissolve in mildly acid rain eventually, thus proving this is a recently made wall.

At the top of the corridor go over a step-stile on the left, and follow the wall on its right side upwards, as signed by the yellow arrows. The path, well used by sheep, deviates a little from the wall along the side of a bank, then comes back right to join the wall and another corridor. At the sign you can go steeply up as indicated to another viewing point for the quarry, a one way trip, or go direct over the stile leftwards by a wooden "public footpath" sign.

Quarry wall

Looking up to the right you see the weathered Silurian grit plates, the natural colour contrasting with the

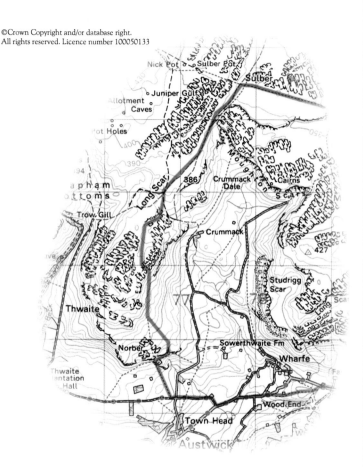

dark quarried rock. The path descends slightly towards a ladder stile in the wall above Newfield House, then it heads obliquely down to the road by a wooden footpath sign, crossing another wall by a stile first.

Norber Scar

On the road turn right, and after a third of a mile just past a partially ruined barn on the right, note a step-stile on the left with a wooden footpath sign. Over this go right across the top corner of the field and over a gap stile. Alternatively, from the road, go a few yards beyond the stile and left through a gate, thus cutting out two stiles. Follow the right bounding wall round to the right, then through a gap ahead ignoring a ladder stile on the right and a bridge on the left. Follow the wall to a barn, keeping to its left, then down the wall again, over a ladder stile then a gated stile onto the Austwick Road. Turn left. You cross Wharfe Gill Sike, where aquatic flowers abound, then Austwick Beck.

Take the next lane right, signed "Pennine Bridleway, Clapham 2". This green lane climbs to cross the Crummack Lane road, fifty yards beyond which turn right through a gate by a ladder stile with no signs by it, heading up the field and eventually following the wall on its left side. Note that the half-buried rocks in this field are erratics, less dramatic than those higher up.

At the top of this first field on the left side cross a stile, the gate having been locked for years, and go up past a small cliff on your right. You can now wander upwards to find and traverse the erratic field at will.

For details of the Norber erratics, see Walk 5.

Eventually you will find a broad green path leading leftwards and upwards; follow this but leave it obliquely right taking a narrow path heading for a high ladder stile in the top right hand side of this field. Over the ladder stile you are on the open fell. You can find your own way to the crest of the fell, which is cairned, but for easier progress underfoot and to avoid too much limestone pavement, find the path 20 yards up from the stile, turn right on it and on the next

Erratic tilted

brow you will see a notch on the skyline about half a mile away, SD765710. Head for this via whichever path suits you, travelling diagonally upwards. The notch is a narrow defile from which the stones have been removed to form a sort of wall on the right side, which makes for easy progress. Through this, if you can find a thin path on the right it goes down into a wide bowl and along the base of a shoulder on your left, then up and eventually joins the wide path from Clapham to Selside. Alternatively a quad track goes straight on to come out on the same wide path: if in doubt, keep going north. The wide and easy path heads north-east, allowing fast walking and enjoyment of the view: Penyghent over to the right and Ingleborough nearer on your left, and as you approach Sulber Gate, over the wall on the right the extensive limestone pavement north of Moughton Scars.

Sulber Gate has a gate, and a stile if you need the exercise. Four hundred yards beyond the gate, turn right on the the east/west three peaks highway up Ingleborough from Horton, the path going along Sulber Nick, a trough indicating a dry valley. At the end of the Nick a small gate is passed then a little way further down a three way sign post, carry on towards "Horton-in-Ribblesdale 1 mile".

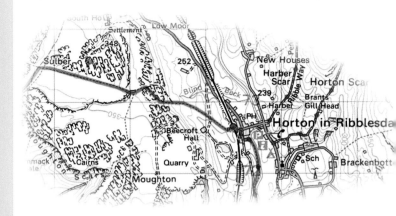

Ingleborough National Nature Reserve
The area by Sulber Nick and north, and beyond the next
gate north, called High Brae Pasture, is a managed nature
reserve. The grazing is reduced in spring and summer to
allow wild flowers to flourish, which has a knock on effect
on fauna such as the rare northern brown argus, whose
caterpillars rather like the common rockrose hereabouts.
A small herd of native cattle, shorthorns, actually grazes
here "most of the year". These are brown and white
beasts, adapted to surviving on the rough pasture here,
and hardy to survive most winters. For more about the
reserve, see Walk 4.

The large path winds down to Horton, and is now marked by
cairns and low wooden posts with yellow rings, presumably to
aid night travel. To your right as you approach the Beecroft
Hall farm road, Horton Quarry dominates the view, and on a
weekday, your hearing also.

Horton Quarry

The large quarry you see and hear to the right on the way down is owned by Hanson Aggregates, and the clue for the use of the limestone quarried is in the name, 80% and more is used for aggregate in concrete, or for coated and uncoated roadstone. It seems that most of the material is dispatched by lorry, although the proximity of the railway clearly helped in the past. The lake's unnaturally turquoise colour is caused by the light being scattered by limestone dust dissolved in the water.

The station is the first building you come to, after carefully crossing the line, if returning southwards by train.

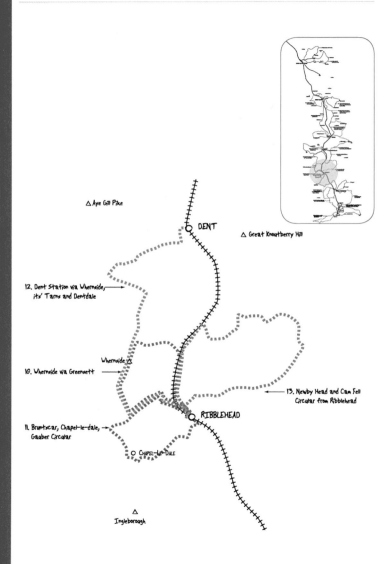

△ Aye Gill Pike

○ DENT

△ Great Knoutberry Hill

12. Dent Station via Whernside,
its' Tarns and Dentdale →

10. Whernside via Greensett →

Whernside △

← 13. Newby Head and Cam Fell
Circular from Ribblehead

○ RIBBLEHEAD

11. Bruntscar, Chapel-le-dale, →
Gauber Circular

○ CHAPEL-LE-DALE

△
Ingleborough

10. WHERNSIDE VIA GREENSETT

Start and finish: Ribblehead Station.
8 miles.   1692 ft. ascent.   4 hours.
Summit: Whernside, 2415ft., 736m. (M,H)
Google Earth: of no special use.

Whernside is often referred to as the least interesting of the Three Peaks, but this route up, courtesy of Wainwright, has waterfalls, limestone features and a wild and lonely tarn not far from the usual route. The Three Peaks route off the summit is eroded in places, but the route along "The Scar" back to Ribblehead is pleasant.

Go down the station access road to the main road, right past the Station Inn and left past the cattle grid up a track.

> **Batty Wife Cave**
> The view of your first pot hole or cave is just below the start of the track to the viaduct. It is an obvious entrance three or four feet wide, but only three feet high and usually with a significant stream exiting it. Not recommended for walkers then, but "a suitable trip after a heavy night at the Station Inn", for cavers. Of more interest is the fact that the issuing water is from the Park Fell end of Ingleborough, via Gauber Quarry.

Leave the track as it curves left to go under the viaduct, to go straight up a bank by some steps, and continue on the made path alongside the line. Keep on past Bleamoor sidings,

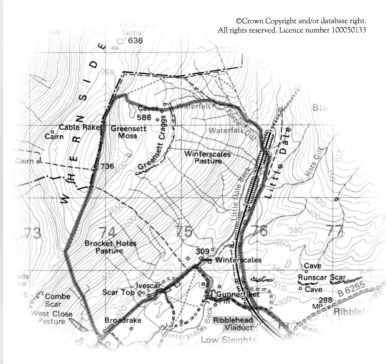

where a loop on the eastern side of the line allows southbound freight trains to be overtaken by passenger trains, then Bleamoor signal box and Cottage.

Whernside from the start

Bleamoor Cottage. Number 3

Although still scruffy, pre-2010 it was much worse, before the owner, Mr. Myerscough aka "Hippo" obeyed an enforcement order from the YDNPA to remove the following: "a caravan, five empty oil tanks, two shipping containers, miscellaneous household items including a sofa and wardrobes, three engines, wheels and tyres various, a small digger, a scrap rotary saw, concrete blocks and posts, and scrap vehicles and trailers". The exit of one shipping container was delayed as it housed a hawk and fledglings! What I want to know is, where are numbers one and two?

The path then deviates from the line and crosses some becks and gills by a choice of fords, bridges and planks, and then the line itself by the Force Gill Aquaduct.

Force Gill Aquaduct

I used to wonder why the engineers brought Force Gill over the railway just for it to pass under the line a few hundred yards further down: it is obvious that if left to cut its own channel on the west side of the cutting it would cause the cutting side to collapse, so the only other option would be to build a channel down the west side till the cutting ended, a bigger project.

Carry on up the main path, admiring the first waterfall of the Gill, until the wall on your left deviates left down to Force Gill and a wire fence continues alongside the path. Cross the fence by the wall over a wooden cross strut and continue

Force Gill in snow

Force Gill in summer

by Force Gill as it curves to the west. A quad track initially parallel to the fence is an alternative to going by the stream, turning to go down to the stream when the northern tributary can be seen. After the down and up over this tributary keep to the edge of the high bank overlooking the Gill as it is easier, and cross the Gill where a wall comes down from the fell in an easterly direction. Just before this, the second, shier and sweeter waterfall comes into view.

Follow the ramshackle wall going up the fell westwards, first on rough reedy grass and eventually on moorland grass, which starts sooner and is therefore easier on the left side, till it curves to the south and you are obviously on limestone bedrock, when carry on in the same westerly direction across some fragmented pavement.

Greensett Cave

If you want to see just how small a cave entrance can be, the "main" entrance to this system (there are eight entrances) is at the top of a small gorge located due west of, i.e. in the line of the wall you have followed up. The gorge is actually a higher part of Force Gill, running north-east/south-west, and at the top end it curves west. The small hole is at the top of a boulder pile at the west end. Do not enter as a slope of collapsed boulders hides inside. Pity, as it is said to lead to a easy walking passage ten feet high and 180 feet long.

The mossy saxifrage can be seen around these rocks in spring and summer.

Carry on upwards in the same line until you come to Greensett Tarn, head for its right (north) end and head obliquely right up the slope, with boggy ground to start with, until the main highway is met again. A gentle wander up the ridge leads to the trig point, which is on the right, west side of the wall.

Greensett tarn

Whernside

This is not a fantastic summit, but it is the highest of the Three Peaks at 2415 feet or 736 metres. The panorama is excellent, including the Lake District seen to the north of Middleton Fell, in turn north of Great Coum eastwards. Morecambe Bay and Blackpool tower can also be seen. Its name comes from wherns (querns, wh changing to qu in the 14th century), or millstones, the summit plinth like most peaks around here being of the millstone grit, and side, Old English for hillside. You have obviously traversed the limestone underlying the grit plinth.

Unbelievably, the summit marker of Yorkshire's supposed highest peak, the trig point, is actually in Cumbria, as it is on the west side of the wall. You'll have to stand on the wall to summit Yorkshire's highest.

Carry on by the wall descending gently at first for ¾ mile, then steeply by some steps, after which it turns down left into the valley, initially down a stone "staircase". Three gates are passed on the way to a lane by a barn, then turn left past the barn through a small gate signed "BW Winterscales 1¼".

> **Bruntscar Cave**
> This used to have the most unusual entrance around, a hole in a barn led into a roomy passage. The barn has fallen down and the entrance is now in the (private) garden.

The obvious path crosses the next field to pass in front of Broadrake Farm and a metal and stone barn beyond. Exit the next field by a small gate and carry on by the top wall of the next field, across the one after that, gates at each end, then the path becomes a tractor track. Head to the right of a house with very steep angled main roof, and a flat roof for its front extension. At the next farm, Ivescar, a double gate has to be passed, then the farmyard and onto a metalled road. Just before Winterscales Farm a road is taken to the right, gated after twenty yards. This is now unfenced, passing alongside Winterscales Beck, over which you pass by a bridge just past Gunnersfleet Farm, signed "Public Bridleway Ribblehead 4/5ML". The track leads under the viaduct and back home via the Inn.

11. BRUNTSCAR, CHAPEL-LE -DALE, GAUBER CIRCULAR

Start and finish: Ribblehead Station.
7.7 miles.   722 ft. ascent.   3 hours.
Summits: none
Google Earth: Not particularly helpful in locating the Viking settlement at Gauber.

Easy walking, mostly on limestone, along the bases of Whernside and Ingleborough. Includes the Ingleborough National Nature Reserve, and finishes with a visit to a Viking settlement and a quarry being "recolonised by nature". Wild flower paradise in spring and summer.

> **Brunscar or Bruntscar**
> Modern maps have it as Bruntscar, as did Wainwright and others, but I note the house sign omits the "t" and research indicates that in the 19th century and earlier, 'twas t-less.

Go down the access track from the station to the main road, turn right past the Station Inn, far too early for a drink, and left after the cattle grid. This track leads up to the magnificent 24-arch Ribblehead Viaduct, and then curves round under the middle part to Gunnerfleet

Ribblehead viaduct

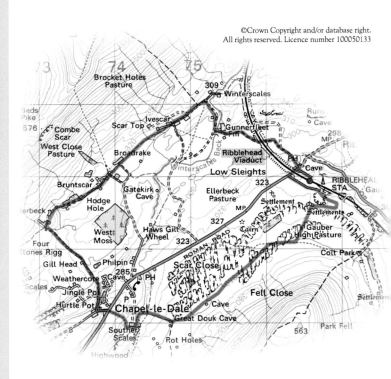

Farm with one gate on the way. At the farm keep left past the buildings to pass through another gate and over a bridge, turning right on the road to Winterscales Farm. Just before the farm go through another gate and at the junction turn left by a sign "Bridleway Scar end 5½".

The road is metalled to Ivescar, just before which another road leads off behind it, which you must ignore. Note the oddly schizophrenic walls hereabouts, they can't decide whether they are limestone or "sandstone", the latter being either Silurian slates underlying the Great Scar limestone seen throughout this walk, generally below the 800 ft (250m) contour, or Yoredale sandstones higher, generally above the 1500ft (450m) contour.

Just after the junction the line of the short limestone scar on the right starts, which you will follow for the next mile and a half.

At Ivescar go through a gate and between the house and a bunker-style barn and through a gate with a yellow square on its post. Take the left hand of two tracks, the right one is marked private. Immediately through another gate and across the field on a track. At the end through another gate and carry on the track, and when over a wooden bridge go half right to another small gate with the yellow sign. It is now a path. At the next gate the path goes alongside the wall at the top of this narrow field, exiting it by yet another gate. I should add here that the great Wainwright gave up illustrating all the gates on this section of his walk "too numerous to be shown individually".

The path passes to the left of a breezeblock barn with white painted arrows pointing the way you have come, and then past a private house. Go through another gate and cross the next field by an obvious path, exiting by a gate. A signpost here indicates you are now on a bridleway. The path from Whernside comes down from your right and Three Peak walkers will be heading down the track to the left bound for the Hill Inn.

Pass in front of Brunscar Farm, noting the sign as spelt and the engraved date, 1689.

There is a cave here, as noted in Walk 10, the unusual entrance of which used to be in a barn, which has unfortunately collapsed and the entrance is mundanely in the private garden.

Through another gate, the track is back underneath the scar. The next barn along, Hodge Hole, beautifully illustrates the mixed stone wall building in the locality. The next gate leads onto a road, across one cattle grid into Ellerbeck farmyard, which go through leftwards to pass in front of the house. The track curves again to the left through some trees and through another gate turn sharp left on a track to Chapel-le Dale.

The Iron Warrior
On the right on the way down notice a wrought-iron sculpture of a warrior. This was placed here in the 1960s, but disappeared in August 1983; somebody or more likely bodies had hurled it down Hurtle Pot, further down the lane. It was found in 30 ft of water and a team of divers had to rescue it. "Time will tell if the spirit of the Boggard of Hurtle Pot will be enshrined in the statue".

Hurtle Pot is passed on the left just before the cattle grid by St Leonard's Church.

St Leonard's
This tiny but welcoming chapel was built of limestone in the late 17th century and restored in 1869, which was when the construction of the Settle to Carlisle Line started. So many men, women and children from the nearby shanty town at Ribblehead for the viaduct construction died of accidents and disease, and were buried here, that the churchyard had to be extended in 1873. Smallpox was responsible for the increase in deaths. Eventually more than 200 folk were buried here and a marble plaque inside the church commemorates them, as does a millennium stone plaque outside, erected by the church community.

Past the church turn left on the road, go up to the main road and across to the ladder stile on the far side. Careful here, as there is little room by the wall and the traffic can hurtle down the hill. Cross the field and the next wall by a gated step-stile, and then the clear path climbs up through a natural gap, curves to the right and goes up to a gate in the fence at the top. Go to the right of Souther Scales, through a gap in a wall and turn left to go past the broken down barns, through another wall gap with a big yellow square on it, another gate, then up the obvious path parallel to a wall to a step-stile at the top. Carry on

The iron warrior sculpture

in the same line till at the next wall the path swings round to the right and up a little gully, to cross the main highway to Ingleborough on a path signed "Great Douk, Bridleway". The path splits and joins higher up, but to see the impressive hole of Great Douk keep to the right. A wall encloses the Douk, enter if you want to.

Go round the left side of the wall enclosing the pothole and up to pass through a gate in the wall further left, opposite the top corner of the square enclosing Great Douk.

Turn right by the wall. After 60 yards pass through another gate and go left alongside the wall on a muddy path, marked from now on with short poles with a green stripe near the top. You are in the Ingleborough National Nature Reserve. On the right is limestone pavement. After a couple of hundred yards go through the gate on the left and continue to the right. This is Scar Close Moss, a bit squelchy in the wet season, ie

Scar Close

most of the time, although there are some stone flags to help in places. Stiles on the left allow access to the Scar Close part of the nature reserve, a particularly good place to see wild flowers on and just before the limestone pavement there, but this is not open access land, and strictly you should apply for a permit (lasting a year) from colin.newlands@naturalengland.org.uk.

Where the wall comes down from the fell on the right, do not be tempted to go through the gate on the right; press on by the wall, now with an accompanying fence, which leads to an area of limestone greenery. The fence disappears: keep going, the path avoids the limestone pavement by curving round it to the left and then back right to meet a wall at a sheepfold. A gate takes you through this wall. Keep going northeastwards following the right hand wall, across a track which has come from the road, and soon join a branch from that track. The next wall is crossed through a gate or over a step-stile, and

Globe flower

after a further 250 yards watch for an oblique narrow path coming from the right to pass through a small gate in the wall on the right. Go through this and head for the gate on the horizon. Through this gate the path heads towards Colt Park Farm, which you can see after a while, but there is more interest to be had if you traverse the open access land to your left to find the waymarked Ribblehead Quarry walk, where definite remains of Viking habitation can be seen. To do this best, head across the moor to about half way to the next wall, then head northeast across Gauber High Pasture. There is more limestone pavement here to enjoy or avoid, aiming for the quarry boundary wall running west/east, with two gates in it, one near its east end, the other 250 yards to the west. The path, waymarked by short posts with green rings, comes out from the quarry through the east gate, south for a hundred yards or so, then turns west, and then north opposite the west gate. It is a little indistinct in places, but you should pick it up if you look for the markers. The Viking "farmstead" is 20 yards further west from where the path turns north and through the west gate into the Quarry: it consists of the foundations of two small and one long building, SD 766784.

Having visited the settlement, go through the west gate and follow the markers east, round the quarry cliff edge, down which there is definitely no way for mortals, then round and down a rocky slope into the quarry floor. This is being "recolonised by nature", but it has a way to go yet. A stream exiting halfway up the cliff on your left catches the eye, and some pools and mounds are there to explore if the need gnaws at you, and of course in season the flowers will be profuse.

The posts lead to the exit, and then you merely have to stroll down the track to the main road and the Station Inn, there being no direct way across the lines to the station.

12. DENT STATION VIA WHERNSIDE, ITS' TARNS AND DENTDALE

Start: Ribblehead Station.
Finish: Dent Station.
8.9 miles   2194 ft. ascent.   2048 ft. descent.   4 hours.
Summit: Whernside, 2419 ft, 736 m, (M, H).
Google Earth: of no special use.

The most brutal ascent of Whernside, which, if you don't like steep and eroded ground, can be avoided by using the Force Gill or Force Gill ridge routes (Walk 10), or via Bruntscar, (the reverse of Walk 10), the latter adding 1¼ miles. A long airy descent of the north ridge via the Tarns, Craven Way track, then up the side of delightful Dentdale on the DW and a road ascent to Dent Station.

Go down the access track to the main road, turn right past the Station Inn and left after the cattle grid on a track.

Whernside from High Birkwith

The track leads up to the magnificent 24-arch Ribblehead Viaduct, and then curves round under the middle part to Gunnerfleet Farm, with one gate on the way. At the farm keep left past the buildings to pass through another gate, over a bridge and turn right on the road to Winterscales Farm. Near the farm go

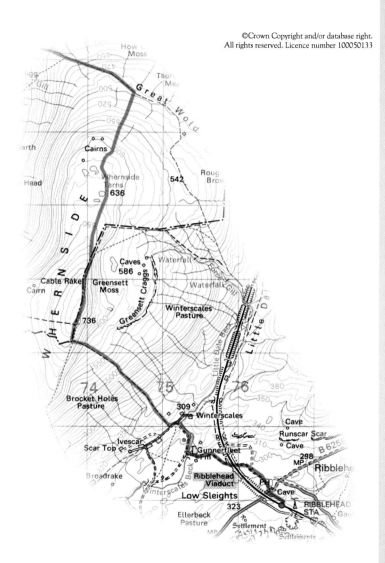

through another gate and at the T-junction turn left by a sign "Bridleway Scar End 5.5"

About 150 yards on this road and just past a wall joining the road wall from the right, an unmarked ladder stile is taken, to go up the field alongside the wall. This is not on open access land yet, but is a long standing "permissive" path. By a small conifer plantation a wall stile gives leads to the open access land of the fell. Carry on up the path to the corner of walls ahead, a long half mile, where the going gets steeper and the path eroded. Follow the wall and fence on the left up to the summit ridge, then right for the summit in 250 yards.

Keep to the right of the wall/fence on the way north down the crest, till just after a wall joins the wall from the left about a thousand yards from the summit, where you cross the fence on the left by a stile, and into Cumbria from North Yorkshire. Note as for the Walk 10, that the summit Trig point you passed was in Cumbria.

The definite and sometimes very boggy path leads down the ridge very gently to start with, giving grand views ahead of Rise Hill with Swarth Fell and Wild Boar Fell beyond, Great Knoutberry to the right, and eventually Dentdale, a particularly good view down the dale when you get to the shoulder of the ridge. The underlying rock here and all the way from the summit is gritstone, hence the peat bogs. Before the shoulder the path

passes the first tarn on its right, then curves to the left to pass the larger tarns also on their right, east, side.

The path then heads in a line for Dent Station, seen now over the valley with its inviting road ascent, down the moor to go alongside the fence and broken wall of the first valley enclosure.

Direct ascent of Whernside

> **Dry stone walls and fences**
> It seems that above a certain elevation, here being the Craven Way track, the dry stone walls are no longer being repaired; it is obviously much quicker and cheaper to erect fences, although the poles will never last as long as the stones, nor are they as aesthetically pleasing.

As you meet the Craven Way track at what the map wonderfully shows as the Boot of the Wold, (at first I thought it read "world"), the scenery magically becomes limestone, and the walking for a short while on good turf. Turn left and through some walled sheep enclosures, and keep going on the track which eventually descends towards Deepdale, and unfortunately goes into more sandstone territory with a corresponding deterioration of the track.

Just under a mile down from the Boot of the Wold, go right over a step-stile in the wall thirty yards from its end, which is by a gate in the track. There is a sign "Laithbank". The path splits down the field; take the left branch which curves round a bank on the right to meet a wall, which follow right to a step-stile over it. Head right to the next step-stile a short distance on, and in turn follow that wall, and a small stream, down the hill to another wall and another step-stile onto a path signed "Laithbank". At the next wall a gate with a broad yellow band on its post is passed through, noting a step-stile fifteen yards to the left where another path comes in, which used to be the DW. A signpost in the middle of the next field indicates where the paths join.

Go on to a gate by Laithbank, and so onto a muddy track. Keep on this through another gate, following the yellow public footpath signs, and at the end of the farm a little wicket gate on the left leads onto a path which goes down to the farm track. Fifty yards down this on the right leave the track through a

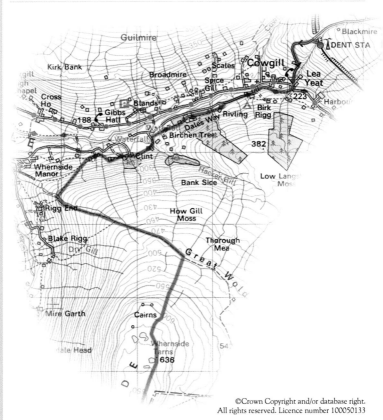

small yard by a barn, and over a fence stile, signed "FP Clint", with a DW circle on the post. Curve right round the barn, over a small stream by a plank bridge, through a small gate, and at the top right of the next field, through a gateway by a barn, follow the sign along the top of the next field, by a fence. At the next wall over a gated stile onto the West Clint farm track, and at the end of the farm turn left down a little path through a crude wooden "fence gate" going to the right over a stream and immediately a fence stile. Pass round the back of the next farmhouse, Clint, then it's a clear run along the bottom of a field to the farmhouse, Coat Faw, in the distance. We're back in limestone country now with a small scar on the right.

A kissing gate on the left is passed through just before the farm, to go diagonally down to another one at the farm, then to follow the farm track left, over a stream by a barn and a left turn. Twenty yards or so down from the bend go over the fence stile on the right, and onto a field path. There is a gated stile at the end, then the field path joins a concreted track to Birchen Farm. Go left down this and across a gated stile at the corner on the right as the track doubles back. Carry straight on above the barn through another small gate into a cleared plantation. The first part of this has been sparsely planted with hardwood native species, donated in memory of Andy and Vera Rome from Ripon. At the end go over a stile into llama territory, carrying on to the left of Little Towne (spelled thus on the house) Farm to the pale green painted gate, into another area of replanted native species, more mature here. At the end go over a fence stile and a small stream and onto a well delineated path in the field, past Rivling with interesting sculptures in the garden, onto its track and down to the road at a gate.

Turn right on the quiet road till just before the bridge over the Dee, where turn right over a stile to follow the delightful Dee till the next bridge. Don't forget to turn left over it to ascend the steep hill to Dent station. It's only 434 ft up, get on with it! Near the bottom there was a chair at the end of one of the house drives on the left, as if to say "take a rest here". It disappeared in 2012. Half way up it would have been more welcome. The wayside flowers are impressive in spring and summer, but while looking at them be wary of the large and sometimes surprisingly frequent wood lorries coming from the plantation at Dodderham Moss above the station.

13. NEWBY HEAD AND CAM FELL CIRCULAR FROM RIBBLEHEAD

12.2 miles. 1728 ft. ascent. 5 hours
Summit: Blea Moor, 1755 ft., 535 m.
Google Earth: of no special use.

A mostly easy walk with good tracks for striding out on, but with a mile and a quarter of moorland, and finishing with a walk amongst the Ribblehead limestone scars and caves. The source of the Ribble visited. If interested in caves, some easy ones near the end need a torch for fuller appreciation.

Go down to and up the track to Whernside as for Walk 10.

Before an aquaduct bridge crosses the Railway, and just before a footbridge crosses a side stream, turn right on a track, which heads for a large spoil heap from the tunnel's construction, with a green metalled fenced off area to its right. This protects you from an old shaft to the tunnel. The path continues up between two pairs of spoil heaps and single air shafts. Note that this track is more straightforward than the path marked on the map leaving the main Whernside path after the aquaduct bridge.

The Bleamoor Tunnel

Joining Ribblehead to Dentdale, this is 2600 yards long and at a maximum of 500 feet below ground level. It took five years to dig in the 1870's, without electricity. The rock was winched up seven shafts sunk from above, and deposited in the mounds you pass between. Only three of the shafts remain, for ventilation, and you pass two of them on this walk and the third on the Bleamoor/Great Knoutberry circular walk from Dent Station.

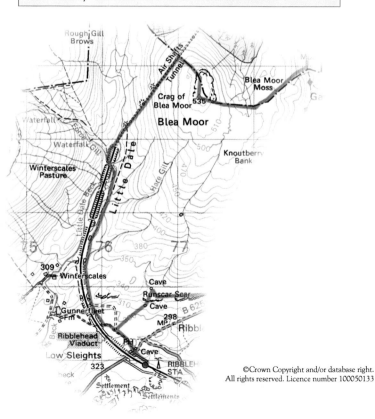

On the Bleamore Tunnel path

At the summit of the path, a fence comes down from Blea Moor. Turn right at the fence and follow it on the south side on a path towards the top. The path deviates to the right by a small quarry as it hits the plateau, and shortly to the left again. The fence and path carry on to a junction with two other fences at the south east side of the plateau, to bypass the summit, which is not terribly exciting in all honesty. Alternatively, for the summit trig point, a path right leaves the one by the fence soon after the last left turn, then aim left(east) from the summit to the fence junction.

From the top you can see to the north Great Knoutberry Hill, and going anticlockwise, the characteristic edge of Wild Boar Fell, then Baugh Fell, the great whaleback of Whernside, Ingleborough, Penyghent to the Southeast, then the Wensleydale hills, Dodd Fell Hill the nearest, just north of east.

Boundaries

The fence you have followed up from the summit of the Ribblehead to Dentdale path is the post -1974 boundary between Cumbria, to the north, and North Yorkshire. You will follow this boundary down to the Dales and Ribble Ways path. Prior to 1974 this entire walk would have been in the West Riding of Yorkshire, unless you took the long route from Gavel Gap (see later), when the section to Cold Keld Gate would have been in the North Riding.

At the meeting of the three fences on the plateau edge, cross the fence coming from the right (south) by a broken stile and

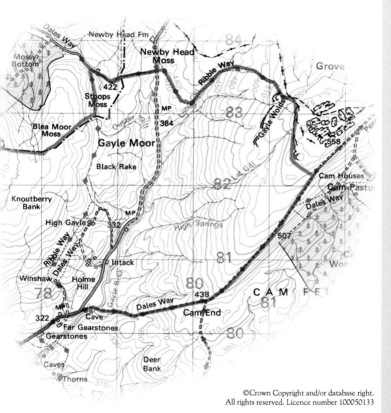

follow an indistinct quad track by the fence on the left, going east. A bit further down in the hollows here, great yellow swathes of bog asphodels will cheer you up in summer.

After a definite dip at a peaty stream the fence comes to another threesome joint. Cross left over the fence you have been following, there is no stile but it is low, and turn slightly left (north-easterly) to follow the left side of the fence on largely pathless moorland, which is not too boggy if you skirt well to the left of two small tarns not marked on the maps.

Just beyond the tarns if you are a dead reckoner map reader (I am not), you will expect to see a fence or wall leading off left (north). This does not exist except for one lonesome post which you pass by on the way.

At the bottom you may again expect to see a fence coming from half left, and some of the posts are visible but the fence is long gone. You see and join the good path of the DW, which go left, north on, to the Dent Road. It is not worth taking a short cut to the road on the right, where you are heading: the name Stoops Moss is the clue.

Turn right at the minor road, which soon joins the main Ingleton to Hawes road . Just before the main road a constructed path of the PBW goes off right, crosses a stream and comes to the main road exactly opposite the gate for the PBW and RW track, which has a much improved surface. Go up this and curve round to pass above the small gorge of Long Gill, wild moors to each side.

> **Newby Head Moss Cave**
> In the gash in the bank facing the road a small hole gives entrance to a "roomier chamber". Another opportunity to see just how difficult it is to enter some potholes, and also an opportunity for clean water if thirsty.

When Gavel Gap Gate appears, you have a choice: you can follow the PBW through Gavel Gap to Cold Keld Gate, then south on the Cam High Road track, or preferably, cut the corner as follows: do not pass through the Gavel Gap gate, but turn right on a clear quad track which heads south skirting the short hill flank on the left. The short limestone scar with a stream issuing from a spring in wet weather, just up hill from Gavel Gap is what most people think is the source of the Ribble.

It seems odd that the RW finishes here, and presumably one has to go back to the road having finished the walk.

Carry on south by the base of the hill. A fence reinforcing a crumbling wall joins you after a while from the hill. When this joins a wall going to the right, and turns to the left, go through the wall going to the right at a gate a few yards on, noting a small black dotted path which starts here on the 1:25,000 map, but on the ground it is a quad track which leads down left to join the PW/DW/PBW about a hundred yards to the right of a gate on the Bridleway. Turn right and tootle down through West Gate, on the line of a Roman Road. The walking is easy, fast, and downhill. Where is that mountain bike?

The Cam High Road
This is the continuation of the Roman Road from Ingleton to Hawes, the part upto just beyond Gearstones being the line of the main road. The Roman camp at Bainbridge, or probably the Roman Virosidium, was obviously of significance, housing a cohort, ie between 300 and 600 men for most of the Roman period from the 1st till the 5th centuries AD. Possibly lead mining in the dales was the reason for such a large outpost. The road was resurfaced in 1751 as the Lancaster to Richmond Turnpike, but closed in 1795 in favour of the lower route via Hawes.

At Cam End keep right down the DW, the Roman Road, the left branch is the PW/ PBW going south to Horton.

There is a ford at Gayle Beck, effectively the Ribble, or a bridge if it is in spate. Go up to the road and turn left.

The Pasture from the Cam Road

> **Ribbleside**
> It is unfortunate that the river banks here, actually of Gayle Beck, not called the Ribble yet, are not passable to walkers, and not in open access land. The walk past Holme Hill cave and down to Gearstones would be lovely in summer and saves walking the road. I remember doing this some years ago as one of Wainwright's walks from Ribblehead.

Here you can trundle down the road, and then up, it has to be said, to the Station, or, to be softer on the feet and more interesting, take a slightly longer walk over the moor to the north along a line of low limestone scars, mostly on level path.

The Cam road and Ingleborough

Runscar lower cave

From Gearstones walk down the road past a barn and two signed footpaths on the left, to cross the road by a gate on the left. Go up the low bank, till the first of the limestone "scars" can be seen to the west. Find a path to this if you can. This is Little Scar according to the Explorer OS map. Generally a good path exists along the top, north, side of these scars, although you may want to explore the pavements above the low scars. At the end of the longest scar, Great Scar, or Runscar Scar according to Wainwright, there are various caves and pot-holes, some of interest to the flexible.

Ribblehead Caves

The first cave/pot-hole you pass is in the small but deep shakehole just north of the clints at the western end of Runscar Scar, Scar Top Cave, but the entrance is prohibitive to normal folk. The Runscar Caves are more interesting, and have three areas of entrance: the first is under the highest part of the cliff at the west of the Scar, a slit is behind some rocks, but in the hollow below a good entrance gives an entertaining six foot walk to emerge again; the middle one is twenty yards below the upper, towards the Inn, and is a wide cave at the lower end of the depression and a slit at the top; the lower is a hundred yards Inn-wards from the middle one, where the stream emerges through a cave entrance at the bottom of a short cliff. This would definitely be worth exploring, stooping, with a torch if the stream is not too high.

Thistle Cave is in a deep shakehole about sixty yards west past the end of the Runscar clints, to the right of the thin path, and with an obvious path leading down into it. The bottom opening is worth exploring with a torch too.

One of the best walking passages is at Cuddy Hill Cave, two hundred yards north of Runscar Scar, where the unnamed stream sinks. Thirty feet down from the sink a tall thin passageway is fairly easily accessed.

From Runscar Scar the path continues westwards and joins a wide green track which meanders down to join the Batty Green Track opposite the south end of the Ribblehead viaduct, turning left for home.

DENT

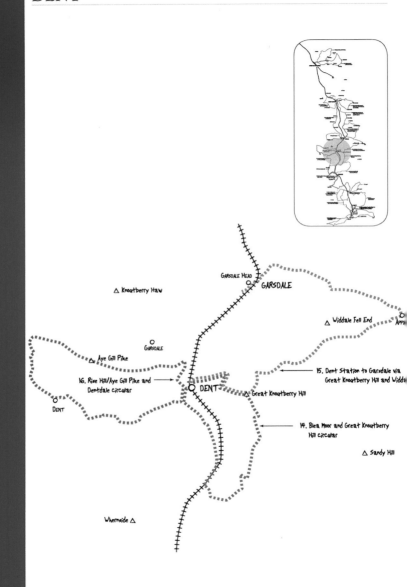

Knoutberry Haw △

GARSDALE HEAD ○ GARSDALE

△ Widdale Fell End

○ GARSDALE

△ Aye Gill Pike

16. Rise Hill/Aye Gill Pike and ——→
Dentdale circular

○ DENT

○ DENT

△ Great Knoutberry Hill

←—— 15. Dent Station to Garsdale via
Great Knoutberry Hill and Widd..

14. Blea Moor and Great Knoutberry
Hill circular

△ Sandy Hill

Whernside △

14. BLEA MOOR AND GREAT KNOUTBERRY HILL CIRCULAR

Start and Finish: Dent Station.
10.8 miles.   2230 ft. ascent.   5 hours.
Summits: Great Knoutberry Hill, 2205ft., 672m.,
(M, H); Blea Moor, 1755ft., 535m.
Google Earth: Of no special use.

A walk with a difference, involving nearly four miles of road walking, split into bits at the start and finish, delightful in spring and summer as the verges are resplendent with flowers and the roads are quiet. There is also a mile and a quarter of rough moorland walking, then good walking tracks and paths with excellent views, and you actually walk some way on top of the railway line (course of).

Turn down the road from the station towards Dentdale, and count the number of different species of flowers you can see on the verges. I'll help by saying that from May there is some common twayblade on the left a little way down.

There are some steep hills out of Dentdale, and in my opinion going up this one on a bicycle is the worst, worse than coming the other way from Garsdale. Be thankful you are going down it.

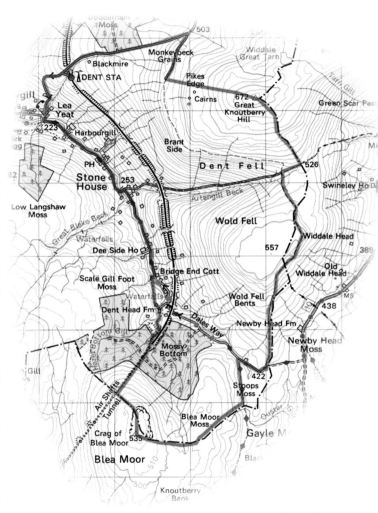

The Coal Road
So-called as coal pits higher up used to serve the local communities, ceasing when the railway came to deliver coal more cheaply. Higher up it is marked as Galloway Gate, a previous drove road for cattle from Scotland to southern markets.

Turn left at the bottom by the delightful hamlet of Lea Yeat, over the bridge and on up the dale. The Dee accompanies you all the way till you turn off: a lovely river on limestone, which goes underground in dry weather, with an unusual bed of large flat slabs and little waterfalls.

Cranesbills
To continue the botanical interest, from June till September one of the commonest flowers on the verges will be the blue meadow cranesbill, but see if you can spot the less common variety, the wood cranesbill. The flowers are a little smaller, redder, more numerous, and the leaves are distinctly different, much less cut. They flower earlier as well, often by the end of May and are gone earlier.

You will soon pass the Sportsman Inn, an establishment I have tried to find refreshments at on various occasions, never with success, so I can't tell you what it's like. The opening times are not for walkers.

At two and a bit miles from the station, you will see the white Bridge End Cottage on the left, just before the road curves to the left. Turn off the road at the footpath sign on the right, cross a grassy stone bridge and

The River Dee

Meadow Cranesbills

Wood Cranesbills

Yardbirds sign

through a gate, turn left and follow the path to cross a side-stream by a two plank bridge, and immediately over a stile. Go up the field by the fence on the left, then head straight for Dent Head Farm seen up ahead. This can be somewhat boggy.

The bedrock has now changed from limestone to sandstone and what appears to be coal measure.

At the farm you will see a curious sign "YARDBIRDS These birds are not dangerous and will do you no harm……".

If you escape mauling by the turkeys, hens and geese, the obvious path continues down to cross a stream by a bridge, then up by the stream with some spoil heaps on the right, presumably from the Bleamoor tunnel, the entrance of which you can see on the left further on. The path passes through a gap in a wall and climbs up to the right of the railway and through a very boggy bit just before the plantation, and then on some occasional boards through the plantation. Half way to the forestry track, in a clearing on the left, Mossy Bottom on the map, you will see some planted broad leafed trees among the young Norway Spruces, which should make this walk a little more interesting in twenty years time.

Some steps lead up to a forestry track, aggressively private, and more steps lead up the other side to climb through the trees, a gloomy but short section, to the open moor where a large air shaft of the tunnel (one of three remaining) greets you. It was actually steaming when we passed, more from the sun heating rainwater than coming from down below, I think.

Continue to the summit of the path, which eventually would drop you down to Ribblehead, travelling for all but the first hundred yards exactly on top of the railway. At the summit of the path, where a fence comes down from Blea Moor, turn left after crossing the stile. Follow the fence on a path towards the top of the moor. The path deviates to the right by a small quarry as it hits the plateau and shortly to the left again. The fence and path carry on to a junction with two other fences at the south-east side of the plateau, so you can bypass the summit if you want by following the fence. Alternatively, for the trig point a path takes off to the right after 60 yards or so after the last left turn, then go left (east) from the trig point to the fence junction.

Train near Bleamoor Tunnel

Air shaft on Bleamoor Tunnel

From the top you can see Great Knoutberry Hill to the north, then, going anticlockwise, the characteristic edge of Wild Boar Fell, Baugh Fell, the great whaleback of Whernside, Ingleborough, Penyghent to the south-east, then the Wensleydale hills with Dodd Fell Hill the nearest, just north of east.

At the meeting of the three fences on the plateau edge, cross the fence coming from the right (south) by a broken stile and follow an indistinct quad track by the fence on the left, going east. A bit further down in the hollows here, great yellow swathes of bog asphodels will cheer you in summer.

After a definite dip at a peaty stream the fence comes to another threesome joint. Cross left over the fence you have been following (there is no stile but it is low) to turn slightly left (north-easterly) and follow the left side of the fence on largely pathless moorland, which is not too boggy if you skirt well to the left of two small tarns not marked on the maps.

Just beyond the tarns if you are a meticulous map reader, you will expect to see a fence or wall leading off left (north). This does not exist except for one lonesome post which you pass by on the way.

At the bottom you may again expect to see a fence coming from half left; some of the posts are visible but the fence is long gone. You see and join the good path of the DW, go north on this to the Dent Road. It is not worth taking a short cut to the road on the right, where you are heading. The name Stoops Moss gives the game away.

Dent Head viaduct

Turn right at the road and after 450 yards take a left up a track, which is now the PBW. This gradually climbs into limestone country again after the first gate. Continue round Wold Fell and down to the track, the last bit before the track having been improved as part of the PBW. Turn right up the track to Widdale and after 200 yards turn left over a good stile with a brown marker sign. Follow the wall on your right up on a path to the summit of Great Knoutberry Hill and a good panorama. At 2205ft (672m), it is a significant hill, being only 72ft (22m) less in height than Penyghent for example, although perhaps not quite as distinctive to look at!

Follow the fence down just north of west to the good track skirting the hill at mid height.

The summit was of grit/sandstone bedrock, but you will meet limestone again on the way down.

At the wide track, an old drove road, turn right, with grand views of Wild Boar Fell straight ahead and the mass of Baugh Fell to its left, to gain the "Coal Road". Turn left here and return in just over a mile, all downhill, to the station and your train if you've planned it right.

15. DENT STATION TO GARSDALE VIA GREAT KNOUTBERRY HILL AND WIDDALE FELL

Start: Dent Station.
Finish: Garsdale Station.
13.3 miles. 2010 ft. ascent. 2073 ft. descent. 6 hours.
Summit: Great Knoutberry Hill, 2205 ft., 672 m., (M,H).
Google Earth: of no special use.

A wild ridge walk with no paths on the map after Great Knoutberry till off the ridge, but on open access land till the valley. Underfoot not as boggy as you might think, and quite good going in places. Navigation is helped by walls and fences; this needs close correlation between the text and map. The walk is worth it for Widdale Little Tarn alone.

I wanted this walk to descend the lovely ridge as it becomes defined, all the way to near Birkrigg Farm, but the track out of the open access land, as for all exits along the entire northern boundary of the open access land, is private, hence the descent east to Widdale as the ridge proper begins.

At the Coal Road turn right, to climb it for just over a mile, then turn acutely right up the PBW, signed with the white acorn and "Arten Gill Moss 2". Six hundred yards or so up as a fence comes down from the fell, a gate by a stile on the left leads into a small enclosure, then a metal gate gives access to the moorland. Follow the fence up on your left, past the cairns on Pikes Edge where naked classic grit with quartzite

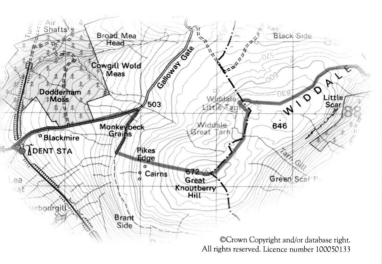

pebbles in it litters the way, to the summit trig point. Here, admire the panorama, then hop over the fence left by a stile, then over the fence immediately on your right, to the two sided shelter wall, exactly at right angles to the prevailing south-westerly winds.

Follow the fence you have just crossed, north of east. On one occasion the remains of a wall helped me here in deep snow. Soon you need to cross a fence with ease, then keep following the original fence down to Widdale Great Tarn. A small path leads round the shore to the right till it meets a fence; follow this to the right i.e. just to

Widdale Little Tarn

123

the east of north until it meets a wall at right angles to it. Cross the un-barbed wire fence easily here and follow the wall down left to Widdale Little Tarn, where you will see the unusual man-made construct in the middle. Follow the shore round either way to the far side where you can walk across the laid single flag causeway to the building, which I initially thought was a hide, but writings suggest it is an "exclusive shooting butt". Nice spot, anyway.

> **Boundaries**
> You started in Cumbria, passed into North Yorkshire over the second stile on Great Knoutberry Hill, and continue therein until Dandrymire Viaduct near the end. The boundary actually passes through the shooting butt in Widdale Little Tarn and along the causeway to it.

At the east end of this tarn keep going in an easterly direction till you meet a fence, and it is probably best to go right, south, to the angle in it (turning south-west) to fix your position accurately, before crossing it to continue due east. Soon you meet a wall with fence atop it, often with a small tarn in front of it. Follow this leftwards, north, on good ground to start with, then peat hags and bog, never in the same league, however, as the churned up southern Pennine or Bowland bogs. In places there is even a path, which deviates from the wall briefly. A fence is soon crossed by some wooden slats, and much further on another one, coming from the north.

As the wall, now broken down and taken over by a fence, curves to the south-east, you see a wall coming from the left. Cross the stream now appearing on your left to follow the fence going roughly east, not the broken down wall going more northerly. Soon you are now on limestone terrain, good walking, along a line of shakeholes on the edge of Widdale Fell. Some of the shakeholes are quite large. The

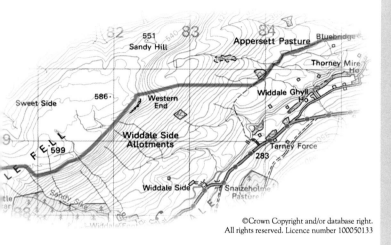

view down Widdale must be good as well, if you can see it.
The reason for this apparent deviation off the crest of the
ridge is to save you from the ups and downs of Franklin
Moss, a peat hag. The first fence to be crossed by the (now
usual) wooden slats is not marked on the maps. A quad
track appears later on, which can be followed if it appears
better underfoot, but keep sight of the fence if the visibility
is poor. A kink in the broken wall is passed through by the
quad track, ie the wall crossed twice, a definite landmark,
then a peat bank on the left with a disappearing stream is
passed and then a wooden slat gate. Follow the fence on
your right, although a quad track going up left comes back
to the fence later.

Where the fence curves to the left just after Western End
Crag, a small crag on the edge, go to the fence and cross it
easily, to survey the hillside and plan your best route down

Widdale Fell end

the ridge of Western End. Your aim is for a ladder stile crossing the wall coming up north-east from the valley, at SD828897.

At the bottom of the "field" after the ladder stile, full of rough reed grass, a bridleway heads for Appersett; a quad/tractor track exists to ease your passage down to the bridleway, but the quad/tractor track only becomes evident if you keep going east by the wall on your left for a couple of hundred yards. It is definitely worth finding. It leads you down due east, to join the bridleway by Black Syke. Here it becomes a proper tractor track, somewhat boggy by and after the Scots Pine plantation. A yellow arrow/white square on a post marks the way.

After Swinepot Gill the bridleway soon becomes a walled track, with Appersett (norse: appletree mountain pasture) appearing in the valley, and towards Bluebridge Farm it becomes grassy and you can enjoy the view of Wensleydale with the classic stepped edges, the High and Low Clints of Stags Fell on the north side and Wether Fell/Drumaldrace on the south.

The track takes a left to pass under the old Stainmore Railway, then goes down to the A684. Turn left, and after twenty yards left again through a gated gap marked "FP Mossdale Head 2M". The path goes by the road to the River Ure, where it turns upstream on the south bank. It is obvious and marked. After a ladder stile it climbs obliquely left up the hill to the corner by some trees, and crosses another ladder stile. A small stream is crossed in the bottom, then the path climbs towards the wall on the right, through a gap stile first before joining the wall, and a couple of hundred yards after the gap stile cross the wall by a ladder stile, to descend through the short wood above the Ure. A stream is crossed by stepping stones at the bottom, then head towards Birkrigg Farm, through a metal gate to the right of a barn, alongside the wall on the right to gain the farm road by a small gate. According to the sign you've only done half a mile since Appersett. Keep on this road/track past the farm and up the bank of Hill Wood End.

After the track crosses a cattle grid it curves left to Mid Mossdale, but at the bend by a footpath sign leave the track rightwards to pass below a bank along a narrow wet field and exit it through a small gate. The path is now obvious through the meadows by the River Ure, then Mossdale Gill, aiming as

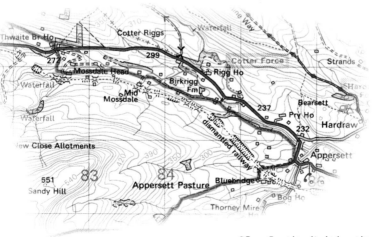

you approach Mossdale Head for a gate just to the right of the house. Yellow squares with white arrows on them show up on the posts. On the farm track turn right over the bridge, noting the pleasant waterfall outlined by the intact railway viaduct arches, then straight on through two successive gates, up the hill to the right past a footpath signpost to a gate through a wall with rather poor post markers. Follow the wall to the right, north, but as it curves further to the right, east, carry on contouring to the facing wall and follow this downhill to cross a stile onto the A684, signed "Appersett 2½".

> ### Mossdale Gorge
> Less than half a mile upstream from Mossdale Head Farm there is a little hidden gem, Mossdale Gorge, on open access land, SD 823914. A great shame, then, that there is no legal access to it from the north, or exit from it and the open access land, anywhere from Appersett to the Coal Road. Viewing is thus a major expedition or trespass. Hopefully this madness can be altered in the future, which will also allow the aesthetically better descent of the whole Widdale Fell ridge. The waterfall of Hollin Gill into the gorge must be one of the longest in Yorkshire. Please note, however, that the sides of the gorge are sheer, and access from the top end is via tricky scrambling.

Cross the road and then the River Ure by the farm track bridge just opposite, turn left and a few yards after the footpath sign pass right through a double gate and head towards a marker post, then a wooden stile at the end of a wall coming from the farm and turning westwards. Follow the fence on the right. Over one more wooden stile, follow the wall on the right and then watch for a footpath sign peeping up above the wall directing you right through a gated gap. Follow the wall westwards; some paths exist to help you, best at about twenty yards above the next two woods on the left. Cross a wall stile by Holmesett Scar wood, then the path does not go as per the map; it carries straight on and then heads up towards the far bottom corner of the plantation, to cross a ladder stile. A small stream defile is crossed, then carrying on in the same direction a track comes in from the left, so follow this. Suddenly you're in limestone terrain and the going improves. Through a metal gate in the wall ahead, across a stream, the track ascends a bank, but just as it does a made embankment leaves it on the left and contours round, without the mud. Unfortunately the bog appears as Yore House comes into view. At the farm ignore the stile to the right and go left through a metal gate just after the farmhouse.

Turn right on the farm track to join the PBW coming from the north, to cross the infant Ure by the modern bridge or the old humpback packhorse bridge. A few yards on the other

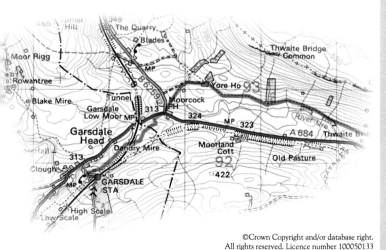

side turn left by the PBW signpost, with white acorns on blue background signs and white arrows, and follow this small made track to the B road to Kirkby Stephen just north of the Moorcock Inn. It might seem rude not to take refreshments at this isolated but welcoming spot, so near to your walk's end, so don't cross the road as indicated, turn left for the inn.

From the Moorcock join the new piece of the PBW, on the left a hundred yards up the road to Garsdale. The sign is on the right hand side of the road. Before the Dandrymire Viaduct, with half the arches of the Ribblehead Viaduct and less than half the grandeur, note the old Hawes line joining the Settle to Carlisle up on the left. Under the viaduct the path goes beside the railway and comes out just below the cottages on the Coal Road. Turn left for the Station.

Hawes Line

Opened in 1878 by the Midland Railway, the owners of the Settle to Carlisle line, it was six miles long and formed an end-on junction with the North Eastern Railway line up Wensleydale from Northallerton. Thus this linked the East Coast main line with the Settle to Carlisle line. Its freight included quarry stone, live farm animals and a daily milk train to London! It closed to passengers in 1954 and completely in 1964, but the "Wensleydale Railway", having preserved the line of 16 miles between Leeming Bar and Redmire, aims to restore the line from Redmire to Garsdale, quite an undertaking as most of the bridges appear to have been dismantled.

---

16. RISE HILL/AYE GILL PIKE AND DENTDALE CIRCULAR

Start and Finish: Dent Station.
12.7 miles.   1968 ft. ascent.   6 hours.
Summit: Aye Gill Pike 1824 ft., 556m., (M).
Google Earth: of no special use.

A slightly rough and adventurous start involving a stream crossing, (which can be avoided by a descent on the road to valley level then reascent of 450 feet up the bridleway from Cowgill!) followed by a long gentle climb on a broad ridge with excellent views. Easy walking on the ridge although could be boggy in a wet season. The return up Dentdale is full of interest, and the walking is straightforward on the DW path.

I've seen it written "it is no great pleasure to walk its boggy length". We enjoyed it, but note, after a dry month and in good visibility.

And in case you're thinking "why not go through Dodderham Moss plantation on tracks, then along a forest break to exit onto the bridleway at SD762885?", it is private and the owners do not want you to.

At the Coal Road go left, to pass through the first gate on the right in the wall, about two hundred yards down. This is open access land. Contour at first and then go slightly down, aiming for a gap in the wall which will come into view. The gap is wire fenced, but is not barbed and can be passed without damaging it or you. Head then for which ever point you think is best to climb the far bank of Cowgill Beck after

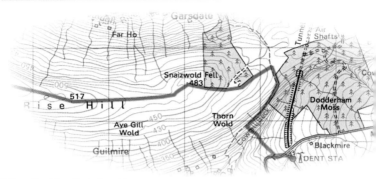

crossing it. Going down the stream gully marked on the map is fine, and straight up from here to the bridleway is not too steep. Where the next stream north comes out from under the bridleway it is easy to cross the solid wall via nicely placed steps on either side, although it is not a formal style. If you head for the forest to cross the stream, the bank opposite is very steep, but access to the bridleway is in the forest, where a non barbed-wire fence can be crossed.

Go up the bridleway, through a gate and just past a bridleway sign go left over a wooden stile and follow the fence and wall on your right upwards towards a plantation. There the view unfolds, from Great Knoutberry Hill on the left close by, round clockwise to Ingleborough, Whernside, an elegant Great Coum and then Middleton Fell with the great bite of Combe Scar taken out of it.

Near the end of the plantation cross the fence by a stile and continue between a fence and a wall to its end, to cross another stile. Follow the wall up the hill on its right side. Note the walls here are all made of limestone, and soon you will come to its naked parent rock with corresponding good turf to walk on.

There are no obstacles to progress now, the odd stile or wall gap, but most walls on the map are broken down. Gritstone appears on Rise Hill, and is with you till the other side of the summit. The sides of Rise Hill are made up of the Yoredale Series, layers of sandstone, limestone and shales, hence it is a classic

Rise Hill from Flintergill

Dales hill, although not as impressive to look at.

The triangulation pillar on Aye Gill Pike, less pike than ridge summit, is hiding on the other side of the wall. Here the Howgill Fells are fully exposed rightwards, and the Lake District Fells loom ahead with the steep side of the Langdale Pikes prominent.

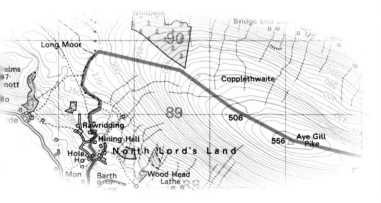

133

There are three stiles to cross on the way down, two gated, keeping the wall on your left. A short passage of limestone turf gives way again to boggy sandstone type terrain opposite the plantation. Continue down, with Sedbergh in view at some stage. A short way up the rise after the boggy lowest point turn left through a gate, or a gated stile, and follow the wall down on your right side. The path and wall curves round to the left, through a couple of gates, and onto a green lane. Through the farmyard gates of Lunds go down the road a short while, being careful not to miss the gated gap with a yellow footpath marker on the left, just opposite the bottom of the house, Hining Hill. Through this go right across a short field to another gated gap, across the lane, down the field left, aiming for where a wall comes up from the barn to meet a fence, here a gated gap gives access to a green lane leading to a road. Left here and down to the Dent to Sedbergh road. Turn left, then over the Dee by Barth Bridge, and immediately left down some steps to the DW path, going by the riverside to the main road again just before Dent.

If you've never visited this charming village, you must, so carry on the road to its points of interest, two teashops and two pubs. Or continue on the DW by the river after a hundred yards on the road.

DENT

A really lovely Dales village with whitewashed houses and a cobbled main street. As the road access is poor from all directions, hopefully it will remain relatively unspoilt.

It has its own brewery, which started in 1990 in a barn a couple of miles up the valley. It produces four distinctive bitters, a stout and even a lager. As it owns the George and Dragon you should at least be able to taste them there.

Before or after such tasting, you can't fail to notice the large granite fountain stone, once the only source of drinking water in Dent, opposite the George and Dragon entrance. This is a memorial to Adam Sedgwick, son of the local vicar, born 1785, who went on to Cambridge University and to be a professor of geology, one of the founders of that subject. He investigated and named the Dent fault, and was involved in the Devonian controversy.

He also studied theology, but upset the church with his forward views on geology: after one speech in York the entire chapter house refused to sit down with him!

On the other hand, he violently disagreed with Darwin, one of his Cambridge pupils, about evolution and natural selection, championing the Church's conservative viewpoint. Being a son of Dent, however, he maintained warm relations with Darwin until his death.

A visit to the church should make you wonder why there is a flat gravestone just by the entrance. It is of George Hodgson, whom the locals thought was a vampire. He

---

died in 1715 aged 94, quite a bit older than his peers, hence the suspicion some other forces were at work, especially as his canine teeth remained his own. When some unexpected deaths occurred, and a "ghost" was seen in the churchyard, there was a general outcry and he was exhumed, brought close to the church porch and reburied with a stake through his heart, the hole in the gravestone being there for you to see.

It is also famous for the "Terrible Knitters", terrible here not meaning awful, but awesome. Knitting was a livelihood from the late 16th century in all the dales, but from the 18th till the late 19th century mostly in the remote dales like Dentdale, as the new turnpike road (modern A65), opened up the southern ones. The Dent ones were rebuked for knitting in church, and even did it on the march.

Either way, via Dent or the river, meet at Church Bridge, where the DW continues on the south side of the Dee, then very quickly the Keld Beck. At the end of the second field from the bridge it is tempting to carry on through a small gate, as there are no signs here, but the way is left over the Keld Beck by a concrete bridge, after which you see a DW signpost directing you along the side of the field ahead. Soon the path becomes enclosed, and leads you down to the Dee again. At the junction of Deepdale Beck with the Dee, the path follows the beck south. Here you may note that both rivers are dry, as they often are in summer, the water passing underground in channels eroded in the limestone, but Deepdale Beck at least soon reappears upstream.

At the minor road turn left over Mill Bridge, then left over a stile signed "FP Tommy Bridge ¼" and up the hill, a marker post helping the direction. Down to the Dee, a river here usually, and cross Tommy Bridge, through the gate and right, along the north bank of the Dee, signed "Dales Way".

> **Upper Dentdale Cave System**
> From just beyond Tommy Bridge, upstream to beyond
> Ibbeth Peril waterfall, the River and its environs are
> an SSSI. A pre-existing cave system in the Great Scar
> limestone of the glacially fashioned Dent valley floor has
> been broken into by the eroding River Dee, progressively
> modifying it. This is evident to you by the many cave
> entrances to be seen, although the majority are upstream
> of where you leave the river. Some caves are influent – the
> river goes into them, indeed most water here is usually
> underground, and some are resurgent - the river comes
> out of them. The river bed itself is a smooth platform, with
> steps and ledges, unusual and always a pleasure to look at.

After 600 yards or so watch out for a footbridge:cross the Dee
again on this and go up towards a post with a yellow mark by a
side beck gully, which go round the top of, and up some steps.
This is called Lenny's Leap, and I don't know why, but I do know
that Tub Hole Cave entrance is in the bottom of it. Go up the
field to the road through a metal gate and turn left. Up the hill
turn right up a concrete drive, there is a sign "Laithbank", hidden
by the stump of a tree. Go up this till the track turns right, when
you turn left over a fence stile, signposted "FP Clint", with a
DW circle on the post. Curve right round the barn, over a small
stream by a plank bridge, and at the top right of the next field,
through a gateway by a barn, follow the sign along the top of the
next field, by a fence. At the next wall over a gated stile onto
the West Clint farm track, and at the end of the farm turn left
down a little path through a crude wooden "fence gate" going
to the right by a plank over a stream and immediately a fence
stile. Pass round the back of the next farmhouse, Clint, then it's
a clear run along the bottom of a field to the farmhouse, Coat
Faw, in the distance. We're back in limestone country now with
a small scar on the right.

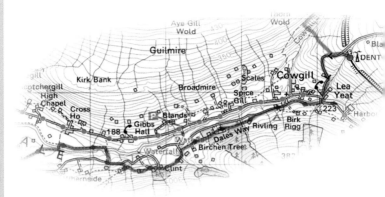

A kissing gate on the left is passed through just before the farm, diagonally down to another one at the farm, then follow the farm track left, over a stream by a barn, then it turns left. Twenty yards or so down from the bend go over the fence stile on the right, and onto a field path. There is a gated stile at the end, then the field path joins a concreted track to Birchen Farm. Go left down this and across a gap stile at the corner on the right as the track doubles back. Carry straight on above the barn through another small gate into a cleared plantation. The first part of this has been sparsely planted with hardwood native species, donated in memory of Andy and Vera Rome from Ripon.

At the end over a stile into llama territory, carrying on to the left of Little Towne (spelt thus on the house) Farm to the pale green painted gate, into another area of replanted native species, more mature here. At the end go over a fence stile and a small stream and onto a well delineated path in the field, past Rivling with interesting sculptures in the garden, onto its track and down to the road at a gate.

Right on the quiet road till just before the bridge over the Dee turn right over a stile to follow the delightful Dee till the next bridge, where don't forget to turn left over it to ascend the steep hill to Dent station. It's only 434ft up, get on with it! Near the bottom there was a chair at the end of one of the house drives on the left for some time, now gone, as if to say "take a rest here". Half way up it would have been more welcome. The wayside flowers are impressive in spring and summer, but while looking at them be wary of the large and sometimes surprisingly frequent wood lorries coming from the plantation at Dodderham Moss above the station.

GARSDALE

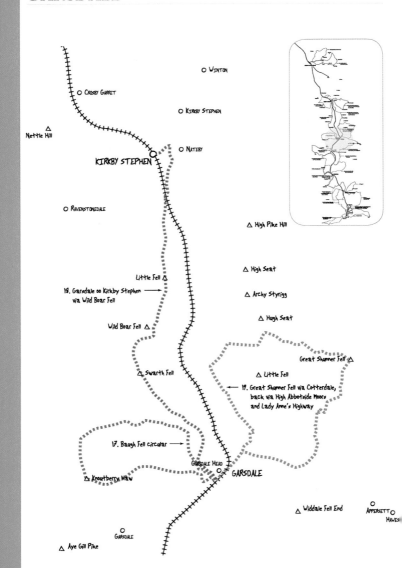

O WINTON

O CROSBY GARRET

O KIRKBY STEPHEN

△
Nettle Hill

O NATEBY

KIRKBY STEPHEN

O RAVENSTONEDALE

△ High Pike Hill

△ High Seat

Little Fell △

△ Archy Styrigg

18. Garsdale oo Kirkby Stephen →
via Wild Boar Fell

△ Hugh Seat

Wild Boar Fell △

Great Shunner Fell △

△ Swarth Fell

△ Little Fell

19. Great Shunner Fell via Cotterdale,
back via High Abbotside Moors
and Lady Anne's Highway

17. Baugh Fell circular →

GARSDALE HEAD

△ Knoutberry Haw

GARSDALE

△ Widdale Fell End

O
APPERSETT O
HAWES

O
GARSDALE

△ Aye Gill Pike

17. BAUGH FELL CIRCULAR

Start and Finish: Garsdale Station.
10.2 miles.   1949 ft. ascent.   5 hours.
Summits: Tarn Rigg Hill, 2224ft., 678m., (M,H);
Knoutberry Haw (Trig point of Baugh Fell), 2218 ft.,
676 m., (N).
Google Earth. Of no special use.

A moorland walk with a fair amount pathless, although not too rough. Guaranteed solitude after passing Grisedale, so a skinny dip in West Baugh Tarn after the long haul up in summer is gloriously possible. Note that there are toilets at the north end of the southbound platform of Garsdale Station, but the only legal way between platforms is to go to the road and under the bridge.

At the "Coal Road," coming over from Dentdale, go down the hill to the main Sedbergh to Hawes road and cross it, to pass through the opposite wall at a footpath sign. Go up to a track coming from the gate a bit further up the road, but after a short distance turn off left on an indistinct path and aim to the left of the telegraph pole nearest the wall on the right. The path leads up the hill and through a gap in the wall with a footpath sign by it, (not the obvious gate further left) and then onto a more obvious wide path, a little boggy at first. The path leads above the River Clough

Clough River and Baugh Fell

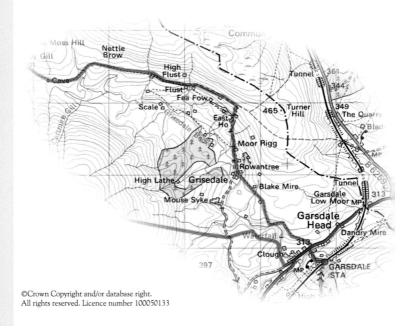

on the left. It is useful here to look left over the river towards the cairns on Grisedale Pike, to familiarise yourself with your descent route from there in the afternoon.

Go through a gated stile and on to Blake Mire Farm, to pass through a small gated stile on the left a hundred yards after the farm. A footpath sign directs the way, passing through a gap in the next wall just down from a barn, and contouring across the next field to a signpost by a broken down wall stile and down to the ruined Rowantree farmhouse. Just past this go over a gated stile on the right and head to the left of the barn ahead, where signs indicate the way through a gate. The next field appears to be a crop of marsh marigolds in spring: join the road by Moor Rigg, and carry on up it past East House. Go through the gate at the top and when the track turns to the right, carry on left by the wall, now on open access land, to remain so until the end of the walk.

You are now on a limestone shelf. The track descends to cross a ford, then through a gate by a barn. Becoming boggy, it continues through some gates and ends at a stile, continuing now as a definite path. This contours past shakeholes and above a small lime kiln and two circular sheepfolds in a hollow. The path curves left round the hollow, and it is easy to miss the main branch, but the landmark to aim for is a small area of limestone visible in a streambed, marked "cave" on the map. There is a small pothole entrance in the rocks on the west side. The path passes through the rocks and climbs a little up the far bank and splits. Take the left branch, which contours the moor. Scan the shoulder of Baugh Fell to the west to pick a route: a grassy corridor presents itself.

When you've had enough of the squelchy path, pick a route left down to cross Rawthey Gill and climb your chosen route up the broad west "ridge". The going gets better the higher up you are, but on a hot day is still hard, and it is normal to see small cairns turn into sheep. You may pass the small unnamed tarn on the now definite broad ridge, but can't miss West Baugh Fell Tarn. Aim to the right side. It's a shallow tarn with a good walk in on flat stones, and most welcome to lie in on a hot day. No need for a costume, no one comes this way!

The view of the Howgills is full from here, as expected. Bare areas in the gritstone give easy walking up the centre of the ridge now, but if you go over to the west edge a good view of the Rawthey valley unfolds, with Sedbergh in the distance, Middleton Fell to the left, then the U-shaped valley where Barbondale starts, beyond the sloping end of the ridge of Rise Hill with a plantation on it.

As you meet the wall of the summit ridge, go left up along it to the trig point of Knoutberry Haw, not a great summit, but you can now see Great Coum across Rise Hill, with Whernside to its left hiding Ingleborough, then Penyghent. A path/quad track now takes you to the true summit of this vast Fell, Tarn Rigg Hill, six feet higher than the trig point, and with nothing of note to mark it.

Carry on parallel to the wall until you see the final tarn, which is separate from the East Tarns, and aim for its right side, then for the cairns of Grisedale Pike. The going is a little rough here, but beyond the cairns down the flank exactly towards Dandrymire Viaduct the going is much better than following the wall. There is one fence to cross, not marked on the map, around White Mea, easily done by a short wooden section. Follow the fence plus wall on the left down to where it meets Stony Gill, and cross the fence where it becomes wooden, by the gill. Follow the gill down by whichever bank you fancy, although as it turns rightwards it is easier to cross it and ascend the far bank to contour to the minor road. Cross the road and go up the hill to follow the ramshackle wall plus fence up then down till a fence blocks your progress. Here cross the wall easily via a gap, then the fence where an iron gate assists. Cross the heathery ground towards the fence leading south and cross the broken wall and wire fence, to head east and down to view

From Grisedale Pike to Garsdale Head

Clough Force

Clough Force, not much of one if not in spate. Choose the easiest line round the bank above the Clough to exit the field by a gate by Clouch Cottage, then along to the main road and back up to the station.

18. GARSDALE TO KIRKBY STEPHEN VIA WILD BOAR FELL

Start: Garsdale Station.
Finish: Kirkby Stephen Station.
12 miles.   2142 ft. ascent. 2384 ft. descent. 5 hours.
Summits: Wild Boar Fell, 2323 ft., 708m., (M,H).;
Swarth Fell, 2234 ft., 681m. (H).
Google Earth: Shows the lynchets around Wharton Hall well.

A grand, long ridge walk with gradual ascent and descent, which can be boggy on the first half. Excellent views if clear.

At the "Coal Road," coming over from Dentdale, go down the hill to the main Sedbergh to Hawes road and cross it, to pass through the opposite wall at a footpath sign. Go up to a track coming from the gate a bit further up the road, but after a short distance turn off left on an indistinct path and aim

to the left of the telegraph pole nearest the wall on the right. The path leads up the hill and through a gap in the wall with a footpath sign by it (not the obvious gate further left), and then onto a more obvious wide path, a little boggy at first. The path leads above the River Clough on the left and

Cairns at SE plateau of Wild Boar Fell

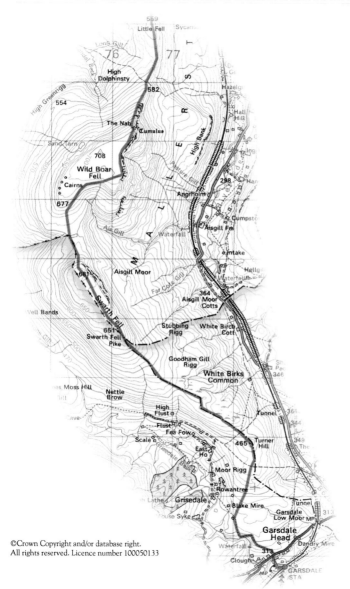

through a gated stile, and on to Blake Mire Farm. Here a sign on the quad track going up the hill indicates the path (to Grisedale) to the left, as for Walk 17, but instead we will take the direct route to today's ridge. Simply carry on up the quad path, this being open access land. Keep the haphazard wall on your left, sometimes losing the quad track, to pass through a gate in the short east-west fence at the top. You will have noticed the sudden change to limestone turf just before the fence, to ease the walking for a while.

The boundary wall on the ridge top is a few yards to the right; follow this or any other path which seems better over Turner Hill. The wall ends and a fence continues where an indistinct bridleway crosses the ridge. The going can be boggy here but you will not drown.

Just before "The Tongue", the fence stops, but the quad track continues on a level, heading towards the shoulder of the fell. It soon finds another fence to follow for a short while till this meets a fence coming up from the left by Flust Gill. At this meeting of the fences a stile leads you over right, to follow the right side of the fence up the shoulder of Swarth Fell.

Boundaries

When you joined the boundary wall leading up the ridge you remained in Cumbria, with North Yorkshire on the other side, which you went into climbing over the fence stile above Flust Gill. Prior to 1974 you would have started in the West Riding of Yorkshire, the boundary wall separating it from the North Riding. As you get to the first cairn on Swarth Fell you leave both North Yorkshire and the Yorkshire Dales National Park, the boundary of which follows the wall along Swarth Fell and then descends with the wall to Uldale and The Rawthey. You will now be back in Cumbria, this part of which was Westmorland pre 1974.

About the level of the first cairn on Swarth Fell Pike a track leads off right, and following this gives a better view over the Mallerstang valley. It runs about a hundred yards east of the wall, which starts after a small dip where naked millstone grit is first met, and up to the long flat ridge of Swarth Fell, directly to the summit cairn. However, in a westerly gale you might be glad to follow the wall.

Beyond the summit cairn there is a tarn, not marked on the map. The main path skirts this to the left and follows the wall down. In the col between Swarth and Wild Boar Fells the wall turns down to Uldale, but you continue northwards on the east of a fence.

Halfway up the slope the main path veers to the right, take this as it takes you up "The Band" and along the rim of the combe to the impressive thirteen cairns overlooking Mallerstang common. When Wainwright wrote about them in the 1970s there were only six, although he did comment that there was plenty of scope for more. Following the fence from the col upwards and then eastwards leads to the same spot, but is of no scenic advantage.

Cairns from Blackbed Scar

Here at the cairns, cross the fence by a ladder stile, to the cruciate shelter, and take the exciting narrow path along the rim of the fell's impressive gritstone edge, with cliffs looming out of the mist on a

Blackbed Scar Wild Boar Fell

usual Pennine day, and if a good day, views of the Eden valley some 1300 feet below. Over to the east is the ridge of High and Hugh Seat and beyond that Great Shunner Fell with a prominent cairn; to the south-east Penyghent looms over the Ribblehead Fells, with Ingleborough and Whernside to the south closer together; south-west the mass of Baugh Fell does not hide Great Coum beyond, with the edge of Middleton Fell further right.

If you wish to visit the summit, a wider and boggier path in parts takes off from the shelter in a northwesterly direction to it. The escarpment is less impressive on this west side however, with an extensive moor down to the limestone rakes of Fell End Clouds, the Sedbergh to Kirkby Stephen road and then the Northern Howgills beyond.

Wild Boar Fell

A prominent landmark from the northern arc, it appears as a peak because of the sharp nab, but from the south is more akin to the flat topped Ingleborough, which is also of millstone grit. It is 50 feet or 15 metres less in height than Ingleborough, (2323ft, 708m) and in fact three feet or one metre less than High Seat across the valley. High Seat looks less impressive from here than the reverse. The name is of obvious derivation, the last pig being spiked over 500 years ago, and its tusk is said to have been found in its killer's tomb in Kirkby Stephens parish church. The norse name has been lost forever, unlike the names around it – the Nab, Dolphinsty, (Maller)stang.

From the summit a path northeasterly joins the rim path at the nab, or you could retrace your steps to the cairns and "do the rim".

The nab, the characteristic sharpish end of the summit plateau seen from most northerly points except due north, is marked at its top by a cairn just after the paths have met, and signals a

sharp turn left wards to descend it. It is worth, however, taking in the view downwards from the nab, as you should see an interesting line of shakeholes.

The Angerholme Pots
Seen from the nab there are about twenty or so depressions along the line between the green limestone and the brown gritstone vegetation. They are all on the gritstone, with none on or below the limestone. Why is this? A similar phenomenon is obvious over the east side of Mallerstang, where the gritstone of The Riggs meets the limestone above Hanging Lund Scar. The depressions are shakeholes, with some having potholes in their bases. Shakeholes are formed by the collapse of limestone under top soil, by erosion by water, particularly acid water, in this case from the acid vegetation in a high rainfall area. Water has coursed down on the underlying non porous gritstone, but where this layer becomes thin near the boundary, it has obviously seeped down and eroded the underlying limestone. This represents 10,000 years of erosion, as the whole valley had its "slate wiped clean" by the glaciers in the last ice age, which is why the shakeholes are small beer compared with those around the world not affected by ice ages, e.g. China.

At the gap of High Dolphinsty, where the PBW comes over from Mallerstang to drop down west to near the Fat Lamb Hotel, carry on along the edge on the right side of the wall which has come up from the west.

Mallerstang
This lovely name is thought to be most likely derived from the celtic Moel Bryn, a bare hill, obviously Wild Boar Fell, combined with the Norse stang, land mark.

The clear path goes over Little Fell and meets a wall which you follow on its left (west) side for 300 yards or so. When it deviates slightly to the right with a quad path following it, take the path straight on and right by the first shakehole. Pass to the right, east, of the unimpressive tarns marked on the map and join the track on Greenlaw Rigg.

The Angerholme Pots

At this point look ahead nearly a mile distant and notice the green wide avenue between two walls leading up the low hill, as you will be heading for this. As you pass the walled field, an oasis of non-access land, on the right, the path carries on northwards to meet the "Tommy Road" at a bend. Go left down the road till it curves leftwards, then take a right on a quad track to the walled avenue. Go up this on limestone and turf and over the railway by a bridge, then down a track to turn left at the road. Up this to turn right opposite Bullgill, on a bridleway to Wharton Hall. As you reach the concrete track leading down to the hall, take care to pass through the gate on the left with yellow markers on the post, to pass along the bottom of the next field above the hall.

The Nab

Wild Boar Fell from near High Seat

Wharton Hall

A fortified manor house, now a private working farm. Built by Sir Thomas Wharton (of Norman descent, as Wh was Qu till the 14th century, de Querton was his name) in about 1436, with a tower house, gatehouse and curtain wall to enclose a courtyard, finished over a hundred years later. It is on the line of the ancient drove road down Mallerstang and in the middle of a 16th century deer park. Halfpenny House, which you pass soon, is at the deer park's old entrance and its name suggests the price of overnight grazing or passage through the park of each droving animal.

Mediaeval strip lynchets (see Walk 1 for further explanation) exist on the slopes on the left leading up to the railway, roughly halfway between Bullgill and Wharton Hall and Google Earth also shows them on the east side of Pump Hill.

The path in the next field leads down to the right, through some complicated earthworks, to pass through a gate with yellow circle markers onto a concrete track, still the bridleway, which leads north to Halfpenny House. Here the specially constructed cycle/walkway leads unfortunately upwards to the station, where the tearoom shut in Autumn 2011. Hopefully it will have reopened if you have to wait for your train.

Wild Boar Fell from near High Seat

19. GREAT SHUNNER FELL VIA COTTERDALE, BACK VIA HIGH ABBOTSIDE MOORS AND LADY ANNE'S HIGHWAY

Start and Finish: Garsdale Station.
15.3 miles.   2500 ft. ascent.   7 ½ hrs.
Summits: Great Shunner Fell, 2349 ft., 716 m., (M,H);
possible for the energetic to add Hugh Seat, 2257 ft.,
689 m., (N), and Little Fell, 2188 ft., 667 m., (H).
Google Earth: Of no real help with the paths.

A long walk over one of the main watersheds of the Pennines, (Eden/Swale/Ure), down by the Ure to start, visiting charming and lonely Cotterdale, up to a boggy Pennine Way and the summit. Four miles of sheep-free wild moor to cross, some boggy but better walking than you might think, then a high return above the south Mallerstang valley on an ancient highway. You might meet people on the Pennine Way.

Go down the "Coal Road" from the station to just past the railway cottages, where the recently constructed PBW path leads along the railway embankment, under the Dandrymire Viaduct, and down to the A684 just west of the Moorcock Inn.

Great Shunner Fell from Widdale Fell End

Boundaries
The county boundary between Cumbria (Garsdale) and North Yorkshire (Wensleydale, or Richmondshire as the sign has it) is just to the east of the viaduct. Prior to 1974 the boundary was the same, but it was the West Riding of Yorkshire west, North Riding east.

The PBW crosses the A road and comes out on the B6259 to Kirkby Stephen just north of the Moorcock, but the short road walk cuts out four gates. Turn right off the road through a gate, signed "Pennine Bridleway, the Highway 1¼". This is now a definite improved bridleway, soon joining a track with the little blue signs with white acorns and arrows of the PBW on a post, to cross the infant river Ure. There is a new bridge

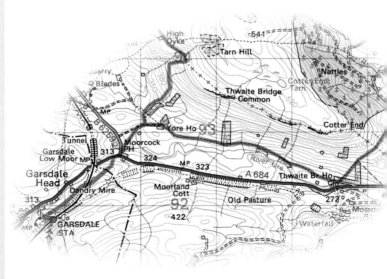

as the old packhorse bridge is obviously not considered safe for motors. Past the bridge, as the PBW leaves to go north, carry on to Yore House, correctly named after Ure dale, which changed to Wensleydale sometime after the middle ages.

Go through the farm yard and just before the house go left through a metal gate and up to a track to turn right, and contour the hillside: there are various tracks, eventually coming to an embankment, before crossing a stream and passing through a metal gate.

Aim then for the bottom end of the plantation ahead, to negotiate a small stream gully before the obvious ladder stile. Continue diagonally right downwards till you meet a definite path; follow this towards the trees above the river at Holmesett Scar. Here pass through a gap stile. A thin path continues towards the top corner of the next small wood, passing a footpath post. The best path now skirts the boggy ground near the wood climbing a little, then aiming for a gate in the right bounding wall by a footpath sign where the broken-down wall coming down from the hillside meets it. Keep heading east by the wall, over two wooden stiles and then aim across the triangular green by Thwaite Bridge House for a marker post straight ahead and a double gate leading onto the farm road. Turn left and after twenty yards left again through a wall gap signed "FP Cotterdale 1 ML".

The path climbs through the short wood and exits by a ladder stile, then climbs obliquely towards the top of the line of trees on the right. Over a ladder stile and across the old quarry track, it continues up to the right then contours to cross the next wall by a gated step-stile. The well constructed path you cross is Lady Anne's Highway, see later. Carry on down a well defined path to the Cotterdale road.

Cross the road and continue down to a small gate, then left at the busy footpath sign down by the wall to go through

Cotterdale

a gap in it left, then follow it down to the river. A path leads across the meadow to a gated gap, then over West Gill by a footbridge. Go to the river and follow it to Cotterdale Hamlet, although when you reach the wall which confines the path by the river it is best at present to go in the field and pass through the broken wall later on to join the path, as it has been badly eroded by the river at one point.

Keep on through the hamlet upstream on the road, past quite a few holiday cottages, then on a track. Ignore the first bridge over East Gill, but cross the footbridge a short distance after, to ascend the bridleway, signed to Jinglemea Bog and Hardraw. Don't worry, you are avoiding the bog. As you enter the plantation you see the first of many signs indicating you are entering the High Abbotside Moorland regeneration and Black Grouse Recovery Project land.

High Abbotside Moorland Regeneration
The signs for High Abbotside would lead you to believe you enter it many times: not so, they are just reminders.

By the 1980s, the heather on which grouse, red and black, feed, had been destroyed by sheep. The estate was purchased in 1997 by Michael Cannon, a very rich man keen on shooting, who decided to change things. Without grants to start with, sheep were excluded (the farmers had to be paid for this), and heather was reseeded as it was found that there was no seed bed. This didn't work, until blind drainage furrows were made with single blade ploughs to create small windbreaks, behind which reseeding worked. That and vermin control, stoats, weasels, foxes and crows being the main offenders, worked, so that there are now 75 pairs of black grouse on the estate, compared with two in 1997. Only red grouse are shot.

There has been an increase in other moorland birds - curlews, golden plover, dunlin, meadow pipits, shorteared owls and merlin - only some of which I can recognise, but I thought I saw hen harriers also.

After you have regained the forest track keep going up, keep right at the next two junctions, till after 500 yards a bridleway sign shows you the way back right up the hill, then a zig-zag to enter the plantation again. Where the trees have been felled, the new ones are broadleaved, not coniferous. This will be a great spot in twenty years time.

After you leave the plantation, just before a piece of broken wall and another High Abbotside sign, turn left up a path up the bank to join a green track, turn left, north, on this as it contours between shakeholes.

This track becomes boggy in places, but leads to a much better one not marked on the map, leading east from just after the second stream crossing the track on the 1:25,000 map, to the PW. The first stream is obvious, in a definite gully; the second one is not, it is smaller, with no gully. The good track is twenty yards on the right further on. If you miss it, look upwards and it will be clearly seen, less clearly from south of the junction. Do NOT go on to the tips/pits; the name "bog" suggests why.

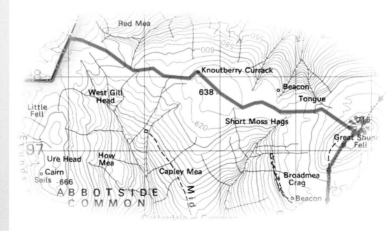

The good path leads up to the PW path under a rise on which there is a large cairn. On the way up, observe an odd square on the right enclosed by barbed wire, with two small animal exit points.

The terrain is now gritstone and blanket bog. Turn up the well used path, partly flagged, partly bog, with some of the flags hidden under water: this is where exploratory walking poles help.

The summit is marked by a cruciate shelter with a trig point incorporated, and has extensive views.

Your way is now following the fence northwest which starts from a point a hundred yards back along the path from the shelter. For the next four and a quarter miles you cross a wild, lonely tract of moorland, pathless on the map. After the first rough descent by the fence however, the going to Knoutberry Currack, a disappointing small cairn now, over Sandy Bottom and the Market Place, is the best walking of the whole trip, and mostly on a quad track.

Knoutberry Currack is a good spot to pause and take in the scenery. You have been traversing the watershed, of course, between the Swale north, and the Ure south. The valley leading down to the Swale is Great Sled Dale, with Birkdale Tarn visible above the Swale. Hugh Seat is northwest, and through the gap between it and Little Fell further south the flank of Wild Boar Fell is seen. That gap is a watershed between the Eden and the Swale. Hugh Seat was named by Lady Anne Clifford/Pembroke after Hugh de Morville, one of her predecessor Lords of the Manor of Mallerstang, in the 12th century. He was a naughty man, one of the murderers of Thomas Becket in 1170.

Knoutberry Currack to Wild Boar Fell

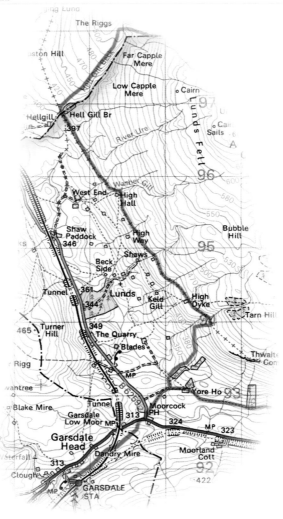

The Riggs

...ston Hill

Far Capple Mere

Low Capple Mere

Cairn

Lunds Fell 97

Cairn
Sails

Hellgill   Hell Gill Br
397

River Ure

West End   High Hall

Washer Gill   96

High Way

Shaw Paddock
346

Bubble Hill

Beck Side

Shaws   95

Tunnel 361
344   Lunds

Keld Gill

High Dyke

Tarn Hill

Turner Hill
465   349
The Quarry

Blades

Thwaite Com

Rigg

...wantree

MP

Yore Ho 93

Blake Mire

Tunnel
Garsdale Low Moor MP
313

Moorcock PH

324

MP 323

Garsdale Head

...sterfall
313

Dandry Mire

Moorland Cott

92
422

Clough

MP   GARSDALE STA

A track to start with from the Currack cuts the fence corner, but then the going is largely pathless and a bit boggy. The time can be passed going up to the Yorkshire Dales Park Boundary by counting the crude wooden shooting hides, numbered presumably for the benefit of the (red) grouse, "the guns are ready at number five".

As the fence turns north, unless you want to bag Hugh Seat, cross it by a stile and continue northwest to the park boundary fence and turn left, following it on whichever side seems best. It gets a bit boggy in places, but never too bad. At a cairn it turns west, and after a small down and up, the going gets easier again. The whole length of Wild Boar Fell and Swarth Fell is seen ahead to inspire you.

There is no good path on the east, North Yorkshire side of Hell Gill Beck, which is the infant Eden, but there is on the west, Cumbrian side, so as you approach the beck, move over the fence to the north side, where it is less steep to descend, and cross the beck. Climb up the bank to find a good quad track which leads unerringly down to limestone pasture and The High Way, where you turn left over Hell Gill Bridge and back into Yorkshire. The gorge here is impressive.

Lady Anne's Highway

Named after Lady Anne Clifford, who travelled it in the mid 17th century, it is at least as old as the Bronze Age and used by all since to go through the Mallerstang valley, including the Romans, although they never paved it in their classical way. It ceased being the main highway through the valley in 1820 when the valley road was built.

Lady Anne, who most of her life was in fact called Anne Pembroke after her second husband, inherited the Clifford estates and castles at the age of 53, when her male relatives had all died. However, the Civil War was still

still raging then and her main home to be, Skipton Castle, was undergoing a three-year seige. The Parliamentarians had the roofs removed at the end of the war, 1645, and a few years later, at the age of 60, she came north and set about restoring and renovating them, Skipton, Barden, Pendragon, Brough, Appleby and Brougham castles, and other churches and houses as well. Her efforts, till her death aged 86, are quite prodigious, but unfortunately her (male) inheritors, let all but Skipton castle go to ruin.

The highway was a major droving route, initially for sheep between the winter pastures in Borrowdale, and the Yorkshire Abbeys for summer fattening in the Dales. Subsequently cattle trade between Scotland and the south, via fattening in the Dales was extensive, maximal in the 17th and 18th centuries, and mostly north to south.

The OS 1:25,000 map would have you believe there is a splitting of the bridleways immediately after the bridge. This is not so: it splits after two or three hundred yards. Keep left for the highway. After the first stream you pass every waterway is bound for the Ure. For two miles the highway, which is our friend the PBW again, is followed slightly upwards from 1300 feet to 1480 feet, over fords, one footbridge, and past two ruins, High Hall and High Dyke, along the limestone seam, with shakeholes on the left.

High Dyke

This ruin used to be an inn along the highway. A 17th century highwayman, "Swift Nick" John Nevison, is said to have been a regular here, although that may just be folklore, I can find nothing to substantiate this. His most famous deed was riding his horse from London to York in a day to get an alibi for a robbery.

Some 500 yards after High Dyke, and just before a lime kiln on the right, turn right through a little gate signed "Moorcock Inn, 1¼". This is still the PBW, curving down towards and along the side of the lowest plantation. Through the bottom gate turn left and soon you cross the Ure Bridge which I hope you will recognise from this

The Moorcock

morning. Retrace your steps to the station, and no-one will begrudge you a well earned drink on the way back, and be aware that they have had their own bitter beer on tap in the past, and maybe in the future - be careful how you ask for it.

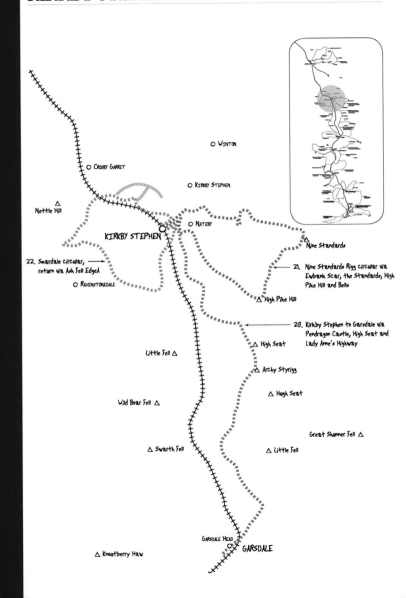

○ WINTON

○ CROSBY GARRET

○ KIRKBY STEPHEN

△ Nettle Hill

KIRKBY STEPHEN

○ NATEBY

△ Nine Standards

22. Smardale circular, return via Ash Fell Edge↑

21. Nine Standards Rigg circular via Ewbank Scar, the Standards, High Pike Hill and Bells

○ RAVENSTONEDALE

△ High Pike Hill

20. Kirkby Stephen to Garsdale via Pendragon Castle, High Seat and Lady Anne's Highway

△ High Seat

Little Fell △

△ Archy Styrigg

Wild Boar Fell △

△ Hugh Seat

Great Shunner Fell △

△ Swarth Fell

△ Little Fell

GARSDALE HEAD ○ GARSDALE

△ Knoutberry Haw

20. KIRKBY STEPHEN TO GARSDALE VIA PENDRAGON CASTLE, HIGH SEAT AND LADY ANNE'S HIGHWAY

Start: Kirkby Stephen Station.
Finish: Garsdale Station.
12.9 miles. 2568 ft. ascent. 2280 ft. descent.
6½ hours.
Summits visited: High Seat: 2326 ft., 709 m., (H);
Archy Styrigg, 2280 ft., 695 m., (N).
Google Earth: Shows where the pillow mounds are on Round Hill, as they are hidden from the byway.

An excellent outing for views, so good visibility required, and as it is all southbound, it is not enjoyable in strong southerly winds. A pastoral start past two ruined castles and a fortified house on an old drove road; a stiff climb to the edge, where an easy moorland walk gives excellent views of Mallerstang and Wild Boar Fell, better than those of High Seat from Wild Boar Fell; easy walk out by Lady Anne's Highway, the old drove road again, and a new part of the PBW to the Moorcock for refreshments before another new part of the PBW leads back to the station.

Opposite the station on the approach road a sign indicates a metalled track for cyclists and walkers to go to Kirkby Stephen. Go down this to Halfpenny House and turn right onto the cement road to Wharton Hall. Details of Halfpenny

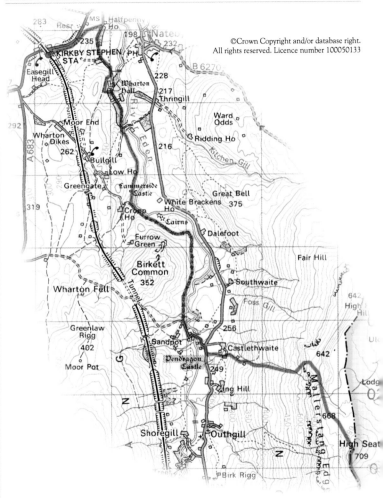

House and Wharton Hall are given in Walk 18.

As the hall appears go through a gate on the right signed "Bridleways Bullgill or Mire Close Bridge", up the field and go left on the second ramp up, which leads up to another gate and into a field above Wharton Hall. At the end a gate leads to a concrete drive, turn left on it and descend towards the hall.

At the bottom turn right by the large slurry tank onto another concrete drive. As you see Mire Close Bridge over the Eden, cross a cattle grid and turn left through a gate to go along the fence on the left. Through the next gate at the field end you will see the ruined Lammerside Castle; head for the gate with a footpath sign on the post by it, then head for the fence at the bottom of the field with the ruins apparently in it. Follow this fence on its right side round the field if there is a crop in it, to take a peek inside the quite small castle in the next field.

Lammerside Castle
Built in the 12th century and converted in the 14th century to a pele tower for protection against those Scots, a branch of the Wharton family lived in it till the 17th century when they decamped to Wharton Hall.

Continue south from the castle to a gate, then left through another gate onto a track, which takes you round Birkett Knott and onto the "Tommy Road" in just over a mile. If you want to see the three pillow mounds (for explanation see Walk 21) you will have to leave the track and go over Round Hill as they are facing the Eden. This is all open access land.

Turn left at the Tommy Road, cross the Eden, and turn right at the main road. The entrance to Pendragon Castle is immediately right.

By the Eden towards Birkett Knott

> **Pendragon Castle**
> Built by the Normans in the late 12th century, it was named after Uther Pendragon, the mythical father of King Arthur, who is supposed to have built it in the 5th century. It is a finely positioned ruin, with a moat into which Mr. Pendragon supposedly tried to divert the Eden, unsuccessfully. The Scots burned it twice, in 1341 and 1541: it was restored quickly the first time but it took Lady Anne Clifford/ Pembroke (see more in Walk 19) to restore it the second time around 1660, and it remained her favourite project. After her death it fell into ruins after the next owner filched the contents, including the roof lead.
>
> The pillow mounds you have passed probably belonged to the castle: a royal licence was necessary to farm rabbits, so they were a status symbol, placed there for all to see.

Pendragon Castle

At the main road turn south for a hundred yards, then left up the track signed "Public Bridleway" to the house. Keep to the left of the house and up through a small gate, then up between the walls to the next gate. After this it is a bit of a grind to Mallerstang Edge, best done initially to the right of the stream, Gale Syke. This comes down the obvious waterfall, a landmark for you to aim three hundred yards to the left of, to pick up a definite track leading obliquely left up the edge, then zig-zagging up to come out where the stream descends the edge. Keep on up the ridge on the right overlooking the edge, where soon a quad track leads you to the top of High Seat.

High Seat
Three feet higher than Wild Boar Fell over Mallerstang, and with a better view I think: to the north of Wild Boar Fell the northern Howgills can be seen, over which on a clear day the Coniston Fells, with Scafell, Scafell Pike and the characteristic notch of Mickledore between them further north; then Great Gable, the Helvellyn Massif, and further north Blencathra with Sharp Edge on its right side. Further clockwise across the Eden valley the northern Pennines are seen with Nine Standards Rigg the nearest, then upper Swaledale with its amorphous hills, Great Shunner Fell, the Widdale hills, then Penyghent, Ingleborough and an odd view of Whernside, like a tipped tent. Magnificent.

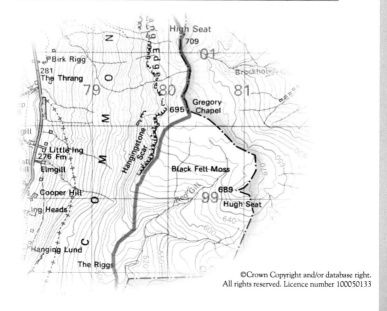

Mallerstang Edge

Ascending High Seat

Descending High Seat

Descend on the quad track then up to a pile of stones on Archy Styrigg (Gregory Chapel on some maps). I suggest that your descent from here follows the gritstone edge of Hangingstone Scar by taking the quad track westwards to start with, rather than swinging left and then south to Hugh Seat, as the walking and views of the valley are far superior, the highlight of this walk. You can also just see the first of the Eden Benchmark sculptures from the end of the escarpment, down on Lady Anne's Highway, SD786985.

The quad track leads eventually to Hell Gill Bridge, where limestone terrain gives easier walking, but first take a peek at the impressive gorge of Hell Gill.

The OS 1:25,000 map would have you believe there is a splitting of the bridleways immediately after the bridge. This is not so, it is after two or three hundred yards. Keep left for the highway. After the first stream you pass every waterway is bound for the Ure. For two miles the highway, which is our friend the PBW again, is followed slightly upwards from 1300 feet to 1480 feet, over fords, one footbridge, and past two ruins, High Hall and High Dyke, along the limestone seam, with shakeholes on the left.

Hanginstone Scar, Ingleborough and Whernside

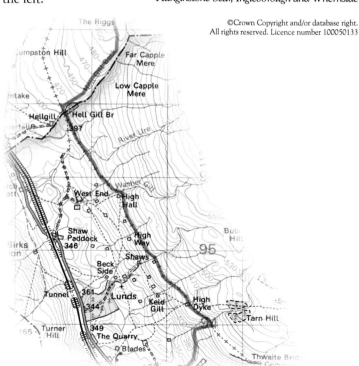

Eden Benchmarks

Ten sculptures by different artists were commissioned for the millennium by East Cumbria Countryside Project, spaced along the course of the Eden, giving visual expression of local pride in the river and its surroundings. The one on Lady Anne's Highway is quite large and is shaped like a river between two stones. Called "Water Cut", it is the work of Mary Bourne.

Some 500 yards after High Dyke, and just before a lime kiln on the right, turn right through a little gate signed "Moorcock Inn, 1¼". This is still the PBW, a new path, curving down towards and along the side of the lowest plantation. Through the bottom gate turn left and soon you cross the Ure Bridge, turning left after a short distance on another new surfaced piece of PBW to the Moorcock for a welcome drink and rest, before finding the final new PBW path to the station a few yards up the road to Sedbergh on the left.

21. NINE STANDARDS RIGG CIRCULAR, VIA EWBANK SCAR, THE STANDARDS, HIGH PIKE HILL AND BELLS

**Start and Finish: Kirkby Stephen Station.
12.4 miles.   2694 ft. ascent.   5½ hours.
Summits visited: Nine Standards Rigg, 2172 ft., 662
m., (M,H) ; High Pike Hill, 2106 ft., 642 m.
Google Earth: Not helpful for the moorland paths, but
show the pillow mounds by the Eden well.**

Poetry on an old railway line; beauty in Ewbank Scar Wood, a site of Special Scientific Interest; joining the C to C route to the eerie summit of Nine Standards. The popular path can get quite boggy here, but over the Swaledale road there is some less boggy and pathed moorland walking up High Pike hill and a return via a delightful green spur to the Eden.

Leave the station from the southbound platform onto the approach road. It's good when you see the object of your day right at the start, the Nine Standards, on the skyline away to the east. Opposite the station on this road a footpath sign indicates the metalled path to Kirkby Stephen, which you take through a gate. Note a pillbox on Whinny Hill.

At Halfpenny House take the gate to the right of it and carry on in the same eastwards line down the field with a wall on the left, and at the bottom go left over a wooden stile and immediately over a gap stone stile in the well, to follow the barbed wire fence north above the Eden, which you can see and hear down to the right. At the field end go over a wooden stile and continue to the bottom, where the Eden enters a mini gorge, only about six feet wide and fifteen to twenty yards long. At the bottom go over a wooden stile and down the steps to the river, which is quite impressive after rain, thundering down under the Stenkrith road bridge.

Brockram

The exposed rock in the river, of which most of the local houses are made, is Brockram, a breccia. A breccia consists of broken fragments of rock cemented together by a fine grained matrix, which can be similar or different from the fragments. In this case the rock fragments are of limestone with a red sandstone cement.

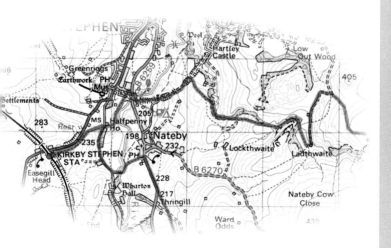

Poets Stone, Stenkrith Park

Go up to the road through a small gate, turn left for fifty yards and turn right through a gate into Stenkrith Park. Take the higher of two paths, ie the right one, passing over the pedestrian "millennium" bridge alongside the Stenkrith road bridge overlooking some dramatic falls, the rock carved into curious shapes called the "Devil's Grinding Mill".

The Millenium Bridge and Eden Benchmarks

Built by the Northern Viaduct Trust, whose initial purpose was to keep and restore Smardale Viaduct, a success, this bridge was to give public access at the southern end of the short railway bed between Stenkrith Bridge and Merrygill Viaduct at Hartley. The "Northern Viaduct Round" from the town along the railway and back via the Eden side is just over three miles. The whole enterprise opened in 2005, but the millennium bridge opened in 2002, delayed by the foot and mouth epidemic the previous year, which hit Cumbria particularly hard.

By the river in Stenkrith Park is one of ten sculptures along the course of the Eden, the second one from its source, "Passage" by Laura White.

The Poetry Path

The first three hundred yards of the railway path is part of a 2.75 mile walk, the Poetry Path, celebrating the life of hill farming by poems relating to the calendar of the hill farmer. The idea came after the foot and mouth epidemic mentioned above, and the twelve poems by Meg Peacock are engraved on large sandstone blocks, two of which are on this section.

The path leads onto the old Stainmore Railway, where turn left.

One of several old platelayers huts now houses interesting information, a little way along on the left. After this, when you see the next bridge over the track, take the path which leads up on the left to a gate, after which turn right to cross the bridge. Note, there is a path leading up rightwards from the railway some way back from the bridge, leading to the right side of the bridge, but this looks somewhat overgrown in summer.

> **The Stainmore Railway**
> Opened in 1861 to service the large iron works in Barrow-in-Furness from the coke plants in South Durham, and to carry the iron back to Cleveland. West from Kirkby Stephen, it curved through and over Smardale and then straight to Tebay along the course of what is now the A685 road. At Tebay it joined the main network. East from Kirkby Stephen it curved up to run through the Stainmore gap, crossed the Tees at Barnard Castle and on to Darlington and Cleveland.
>
> There was a passenger service, until the Kirkby Stephen to Tebay part closed in 1952. When steelmaking died a death in 1962 the whole line closed, except the short section from Hartley (Merrygill Viaduct) to the separate branch from the line north-west of Kirkby Stephen, which goes north to Appleby. This remained to service Hartley Quarry till 1975.

The track over the bridge is double. Use the right channel, through a gate, up alongside the wall on the left, at the start of which you see for the first time a white "Discover Eden" sign with a washed out Kingfisher logo on it on a post. Go over a fence stile at the top to a green lane, and over a gap stile in the wall at the end, continuing on a broad green lane. Pass though a gate or a gap stile in the wall at the end, noticing a sturdy barn in the field on the right. Turn left over a fence stile or through a small metal gate, to go down left to a stream in the wood. The path leads down to Ladthwaite Beck, running at the bottom of Ewbank Scar. The beck soon becomes an impressive water slide after rain, and the path correspondingly muddy.

> **Ewbank Scar**
> This was caused by a vertical crust movement millions of years ago, thrusting the far side up to form the limestone cliff you see, with the beck running along the bottom. The wood is a site of Special Scientific Interest, being an ancient, semi-natural wood. Ramsons are dominant over bluebells in spring, and there are some uncommon plants and a variety of birds, including the redstart, spotted flycatcher and great spotted woodpecker, and the rare northern brown argus butterfly.

The path climbs away from the beck and leaves the wood at a bridge. Go through two gates or a stile and a gate, and climb the field towards another waymarked pole, with the trees on your left. At the top of the hill you see the Nine Standards again. The clear path descends to Ladthwaite Beck again and curves round the base of Birkett Hill, crossing a stile into a field with Ladthwaite ahead. Just before the farm, cross over the bridge on your left and head right alongside the beck, to a gate leading to the farm track. Turn left. The path marked on the OS maps on the right travelling up to the end of the road from Hartley does not appear to exist, although the

Ewbank Scar

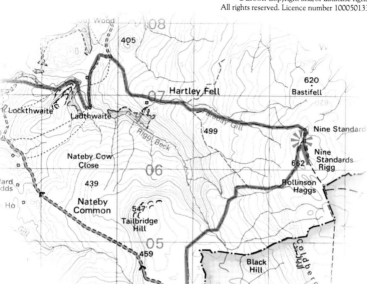

old lead mine, marked "shaft (dis)" and "workings(disused)" clearly do. There was a lead smelt-mill at Hartley from 1750. So continue on the metalled road till it meets the road from Hartley at its end, where go through a small gate on the right with a curved arrow sign on it, up the bank to join a track at a gate. Through

Ewbank Scar

this you are now on Wainwright's C to C route, which can be comforting on a day with no visibility, as you could hardly fail to miss the route to the Standards, but means you will not be alone, and it can be very muddy from the substantial traffic it now takes.

Carry on up the old coal miners' track, (the coal used to be dug out of the peat at what is now marked as Quarry (dis), on the Explorer map, but Wainwright, who can usually be trusted, marked as old coal pits in his pictorial guide), noting a bronze print of a wild boar on a post on the right. This is because you can, on a clear day, see the characteristic escarpment of Wild Boar Fell from here to the southwest.

Turn left off the track at the second footpath sign, indicating a permissive path to the summit (for the C to C). It is interesting to be called permissive, when it is in Open Access Land. Prior to this, another sign explained how re-routing of the C to C had occurred to prevent erosion. This path is marked as a tiny one on the Explorer OS map, but now obviously quite significant, which leads after some mud and the crossing of Faraday Gill, to the Nine Standards. These large cairns do make a misty walk suddenly come to life. This path certainly did not exist in 1977 when we did the great walk, and what a difference fame has made: we didn't see another walker the entire trip.

> ### The Nine Standards
> I can only reiterate what many have said about the standards: that the name existed on maps over four hundred years ago, but the current cairns, which have had major recent repairs, are probably around two hundred years old.
>
> The major use of the cairns was as the site of ritual burning of the author's ancient low slung ex-army rucsack, which fell to pieces here on our 1977 C to C walk.

Having looked and taken in the fine situation, stroll south about a hundred yards to a viewfinder cairn and for the summit take the left of the two paths from here for another three hundred yards to the trig point. However, note that from here south west is very boggy, so preferably go back to the viewfinder and take the right path heading just west of south, which was the original C to C path up from Kirkby Stephen. This does get a bit soggy now and then, but leads eventually to a signpost at the splitting of the way: right was the original way up, left down to the Nateby/ Swaledale road. Both are marked "Coast to Coast". Take the left, which improves underfoot, down to Dukerdale, where after crossing Rigg Beck (which is Ladthwaite Beck lower down), go straight up the slope. You could shorten the walk here by going right, by the wall, up to Tailbridge Hill and down the shoulder to the B6270.

The path turns 45 degrees to the left at an obvious dividing line between limestone on your right and moorland (grit) on your left and continues to the B6270. Here you will see that this path is the recommended way for the C to C from December to April.

The aim now is to get to the green spur of Great Bell, just beyond "Bells" on the map. This is a delightful, easy route down to the valley with excellent views, better than the pathless bogs of Foul Gutter. Climb the good track to High Pike Hill by going straight across the road on a path to join it. At the summit retrace your steps to the small col and turn northwest on a sheep path, which improves as you see the quarry and leads you to the left end of it. You will see down the bank ahead a good path leading on down

The Nine Standards

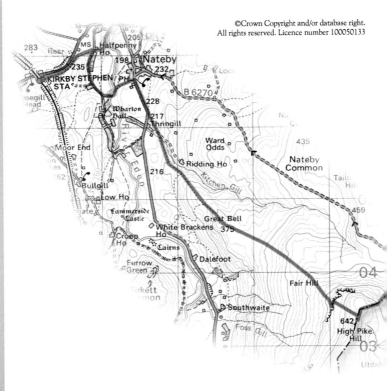

the spur, but if you don't fancy a direct descent to it a good
path leads left to a further track going obliquely down the
bank.

In fact there are a variety of paths down the spur, all good
walking with excellent views of the Eden Valley and the Lake
District hills ahead.

At the top of the first summit there is a curious trench or
trough in the limestone and on the second summit you
will pick up an excellent path taking you down gradually

to the valley. A trip over to the left side of Great Bell is recommended, however, to see the three "Giant's Graves" ie pillow mounds on the side of Round Hill over the Eden. For explanation of pillow mounds see Walk 22 .

The open access land ends at a stile/gate through a wall, and the path runs above the stream, which has had "Beck" added to its "Gill", Thringill Beck, named after the farm lower down. At the next small gate, take the path straight up a small hump ahead, with some workings on the left. This leads through a gate at the other side, then along and over a small bridge and obviously left to the road, going to the right of a large oak tree by a wall junction.

Turn right on the road, the B6259. Look at your watch. What time is your train? It will not take you 40 minutes from here to the station. The Black Bull at Nateby is open till 2.30, and from 6pm, so carry on into Nateby if you want. Otherwise, after about 500 yards on the road, until just after the motor and agricultural buildings on the left, go up a step-stile left in the wall signed to Wharton Hall. Follow the footpath sign across the first field. The correct line takes you through another field by two gates, but if you have strayed too far right two fence stiles from another path lead to the same place. To follow the signs down to the river, keep going upstream by the bank, curving round and through the kissing gate, and over the obvious bridge across the Eden. Go up the field after the bridge to the signposts, to turn right on the bridleway, a concrete track. At Halfpenny House turn left on the track you came on to this point, and hopefully your train.

Pillow mounds from Great Bell

22. SMARDALE CIRCULAR, RETURN VIA ASH FELL EDGE

**Start and Finish: Kirkby Stephen Station.
11 miles.   1595 ft. ascent.
4½ hours. Add half an hour for the full wood
deviation and maybe an hour if Waitby/Greenriggs
Reserve is visited.
Summit: Ash Fell 1263 ft., 385m.
Google Earth: helps locate the pillow mounds in
southern Smardale.**

A fairly easy walk with a pleasant pastoral approach to Smardale, where a disused railway leads through a lovely gorge and nature reserve, best visited in spring or summer for the flowers and butterflies. A deviation to a special reserve of orchids is possible. A limestone upland with a little heather bashing leads to a splendid promenade with good views. Involves nearly two miles of road walking.

Take the main road to Kirkby Stephen, a handy path appearing on the left verge at the corner. By the Welcome to Kirkby Stephen sign, turn left up a track signed "Ash Fell". Immediately you see two lime kilns.

After the first gate you see a stand of coniferous trees with a ladder stile entering it to the left. Go over this and exit by another one at the end. In the next field observe the C to C path going diagonally across it, marked by a post. You join this at a gap stile over a wall at the top, carrying on towards, but not through, the tunnel under the parent railway through

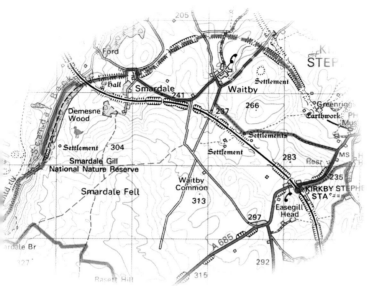

which it passes to Orton and Shap. Instead, turn right before the tunnel and go through the gateway at the bottom, and up the next field. On top of the hill where the Pennines loom ahead, pick out the gate down at the far right of the field, leading to a road. Go right here and left at the first junction to pass by the hamlet of Waitby, then quickly left, following the signs for Smardale.

Waitby School

You pass this building between Smardale and Waitby, built in 1680 and rebuilt in 1867. It closed in the 1920s as a school, but continued as the village hall till the 1950s. It is now a luxury holiday home.

Waitby/Greenriggs Nature Reserve
If you are interested in orchids, a deviation at Waitby to this reserve is thoroughly recommended, adding less than a mile to the walk. At the Waitby Junction go half right and when the old Stainmore railway bridge appears after 800 yards, go over a stile on the right before it and down to the reserve, which is the railway cutting here, to see a variety of orchids: the fly orchid usually marked with white sticks on the sides of the embankment, and many and confusing marsh, common spotted and fragrant orchids, and common twayblade. June and July are the best months. On the return, go under the road on the old railway and follow it westwards through many gates and down to several tracks and back till you are forced up to the road at Smardale.

Note, the south-east end of the reserve is at SD 762080, and there is no exit or entrance here.

If you're not visiting the reserve, turn right past the the Waitby School building along School Lane, which passes near the railway and down to pass the turn to Smardale hamlet on the left, where you go right over the disused railway. On the way down notice the grand-looking hall.

Smardale Hall
Built in the 15th and 16th century, actually in the Scottish baronial style, though the four-turreted west wing somehow looks French. Smardale derives its name from words meaning either valley of butter or of clover.

Turn left at the road junction and left again down a track by a carpark to join the disused railway track by a sign board, explaining about Smardale Gill Nature Reserve. You could

Northern Marsh orchid (left) and Fly orchid (right) at Greenriggs

walk the next section of nearly two miles on the level course of the old Stainmore Railway, but just after passing under the Settle to Carlisle line I recommend a deviation, to descend into the National Nature Reserve wood by a stile or gate on the right. The permissive path descends to the river, turns left for a bit and then climbs back, allowing you to see rare butterfly orchids and if you're lucky, "common" wintergreen. The non-permissive path carrying on by the river is not barred, however, and delightfully follows the river to zig-zag back to the trail just before the Gill Viaduct.

For more reading about the Stainmore Railway, see Walk 21.

Smardale Viaduct
Built between 1870 and 1875 as part of the Settle to Carlisle line, it therefore came into existence over ten years after the Stainmore line it crosses. It has twelve arches of limestone, with grit or sandstone for the edges of the arches and the parapet. It is the highest viaduct on the Settle to Carlisle line, at over 130 feet.

Smardale Gill National Nature Reserve

Owned and run by the Cumbria Wildlife Trust, which first purchased land here in 1978, it became a national nature reserve in 1997 and a Site of Special Scientific Interest. The old railway line was bought from British Rail in 1991, who had wanted to destroy the Gill Viaduct, as this was cheaper than restoration. This prompted the formation of the Northern Viaduct Trust, who restored the viaduct in 1992, allowing this glorious walk.

The woods at the northern end are not claimed to be ancient, although they may be, and in them and around are some rare plants, particularly some rare orchids, I can vouch for the butterfly orchid down in the wood, but herb paris, broad-leaved helleborine, rock rose, common wintergreen, bloody cranesbill and bird's eye primrose can be seen, the latter two towards the southern end. The rare butterflies, Scotch Argus and the Northern Brown Argus, can be seen in late summer.

When the line emerges from the woods it crosses the scenic Smardale Gill Viaduct, and then passes some quarries and two lime kilns.

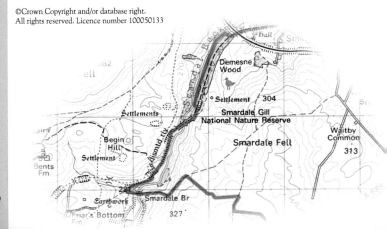

Smardale Gill Viaduct

Altogether more scenic than the last viaduct, this was built in 1860, obviously for a double track, although the line so far has been single track width, and the viaducts further east are single track. The architect overdid it a bit! Built of sandstone, unlike the Smardale Viaduct, it has fourteen arches to span the Scandal Beck Valley. Apart from the major 1992 restoration noted above, further work was needed in 2010 after the severe winter.

The Smardale lime kilns

Built to take advantage of the Tebay to Darlington line, supplying lime for the steel works at Barrow as well as Darlington. The quality of the lime was not considered good enough, however, and the kilns ceased to operate before the nineteenth century was out.

After the lime kilns, a gate is passed, and then the disused railway cottage on the right; now it appears a home for birds. Just past the stone bridge ahead, turn up the left bank, by a footpath sign, over a stile and turn right, signed here "C to C". This wide green path goes along by the railway, and then curves down left to cross the Smardale Bridge, an old packhorse bridge over Scandal Beck.

Smardale Gill viaduct

As you come down the hill, look out for the lynchets on the field directly south,

Smardale lime kiln

*Butterfly orchid (left) and Common spotted orchid (centre) and
Birdseye Primrose (right) at Smardale wood.*

beyond and to the right of the bridge. Over the bridge, carry
on in the same direction on the "Public Bridleway, Kirkby
Stephen". Through a gate the bridleway swings left up the
hill, and if you look carefully over the wall you will to see
the Pillow Mounds marked on the map. In late May and
June this path has many birdseye primroses on its banks.

> **Pillow Mounds**
> Most authorities think that these are structures built to
> house rabbits, introduced as a farmed food by the Normans.
> These rabbits were a wee bit delicate and needed help to
> burrow and hide away from the nasty northern weather
> and foxes. The warrens, for that's what they were, are
> rectangular, a few feet high, varying between 30 and 60
> feet long by 12 to 20 feet wide, with ditches around them.
> They are also called Giants' Graves locally. Actually best
> seen from across the valley above the railway building,
> and best of all on Google Earth, where at least six of them
> can be seen here.

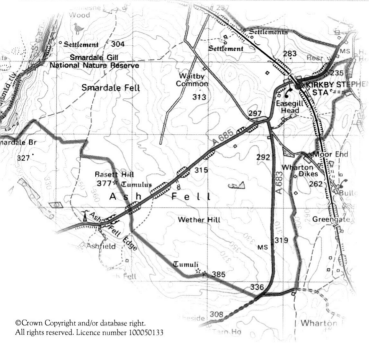

Through the next gate turn right and follow the wall. There is a track, a bit boggy in winter as the animals have taken shelter here from the south-westerlies. As a new wall joins it from the left, follow this due east till a bridleway is met passing north-south at a gate. Go through the gate and follow the bridleway up the gentle hill, nearly to the top, then turn left over the moor through an area free of heather. If it's grown back, you'll just have to bash through. Aim just to the right of the southern wall of the rectangular enclosure, with a large tree just inside it, and from the far end of the enclosure aim up the slope south-easterly by the easiest passage, towards the resting lion appearance of a tumulus at the top. Here head down towards the road, some animal tracks helping,

Ash Fell Edge, towards High Seat

aiming for a gate about a hundred yards right of where the wall on the left hits the road wall.

Cross the A685 carefully, to pass through the gate opposite and follow the green quad track in the general direction of Wild Boar Fell in the distance, and where this meets the junction of two walls go through the wall on the right by a gate. This is where the old thoroughfare from Ravenstonedale to Kirkby Stephen came before the road was built. Turn left to follow the wall on a track over Ash Fell. Almost immediately a well preserved lime kiln appears by a memorial cairn. The walking is a pleasure, on close cropped turf. The views are grand, dominated by Wild Boar Fell with the sharp Nab at the end of its plateau, with the "Appleby Fair Gap" to its right. This is where there is usually a huge temporary camp of horse-drawn caravans on their way to the fair, by the A683 on Cote Moor, every year from late May till the end of the first week in June. Don't expect the local pubs to be open then. To the right are the northern Howgills with the Lune valley gap further right and the eastern Lake District fells in the distance.

As you pass the next cairn the track cuts a corner to meet the wall further on after it has deviated to near the summit of Windy Hill. The obvious tarn to the south, unnamed by the Ordnance Survey, is known as Tarnmire, although really that name belongs to the mire to the east of it.

All too soon this fine promenade is over, as you go down to join the A683. Turn left over the cattle grid and right down the Tommy Road, which name I'm sorry I can tell you nothing about. Over the next cattle grid turn left and follow the wall northwards. After nearly a mile you pass a barn on the right. Here make your way to the corner of the wall on the right, to find a track which passes between the reedy grass and through a gate to a minor road. Turn right on this and then left through a gate before the Moor End farmhouse, signed "Halfpenny House". Aim for the stile at the far right corner of the field, then directly for the railway, which you follow north after crossing a stile to the side of its embankment. Pass under the railway, then over a fence by a stile to follow the yellow arrow direction, towards another post marked with a yellow arrow to the left of a depression. Follow the direction marked down to a fence, but look to the right and you will see some curious troughs and embankments coming over and down the facing small hill. They are the wrong orientation for lynchets. At the fence ignore the gate, cross a stile 70 yards to the right. Here there has been some messy disturbance made and the path may not be clear, so it's best to turn right by the fence till you can easily descend and cross the stream which has just emerged from a spring, then up to join the obvious track. This passes through a gate to the left of the trees and joins the minor, concrete, road from Wharton Hall. Go left to Halfpenny House and left up the frustrating hill to the station.

Wintergreen, Smardale Wood

Common Rock-rose, Smardale

APPLEBY-IN-WESTMORLAND

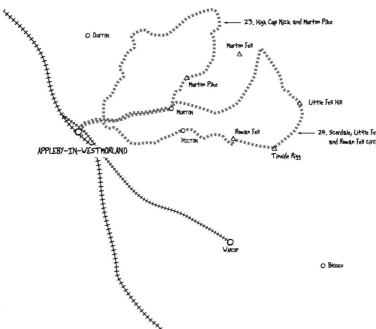

23. HIGH CUP NICK AND MURTON PIKE

Start and Finish: Appleby Station.
13 miles.   2618 ft. ascent.
6½ hours, (excluding visit to winery).
Summits: Northern summit of Murton Fell, 2207 ft.,
673m.; Murton Pike, 1948 ft., 594m.
Google Earth: of no special use.

Although it may look a long way to High Cup Nick from Appleby, this is a relatively easy walk through the delightful Flakebridge Wood, noted for bluebells in May, and farmland to get to the impressive rock scenery itself. Only a small amount of rough moorland on the side of Murton Fell to negotiate. A visit to Cumbria's only winery and art/geology exhibition is recommended, as it is right on the route. The panorama from Murton Pike is superb.

From the north platform on the station go down to the road and turn up it, to the right. As it curves to the right carry straight on to a marked footpath, over a stile and across the busy A66 dual carriageway, the Appleby bypass. There is an amusing stagger in the central reservation wires if you haven't the energy to step a foot over them. Across another stile into Roman Road, called so for obvious reasons, and straight on over another stile into a field, heading for a gate at the far end. Through this turn right into Hungriggs Lane, and just before it joins Roman Road, go left over a stile into Stank Lane, a delightful path in spring but can be overgrown in summer, definitely not for shorts-clad legs then.

At the bottom go over a stile into a field, following its left side till the path swings diagonally right across it after 200 yards.

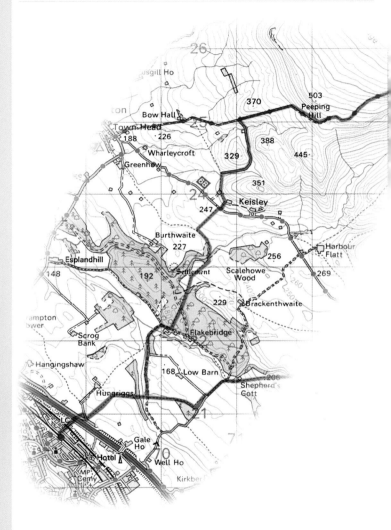

Another stile is crossed at the far side and then in a few yards another stile on the left leads into Stank Wood. A steep path with steps leads through the wood, to cross a stile onto a grassy bank. Follow this to the signpost where turn left, and follow the right side of the valley till the path swings right through a gate, then goes over another bridge and heads for the gate into Flakebridge Wood. Turn right. A sign here says you are on Well House Road. Take the upper of two tracks and just after the second of two tracks from the right joins your track, a footpath sign on the left indicates your route up a narrow path at right angles to the track. You might think from the map that the wood

was all plantation, but is not: this middle part is deciduous wood, with many old oaks and is carpeted with bluebells in May. One of the best woods for them in the north.

There are markers at key points, Turn left at a pheasant compound, cross a track and along a track signed Keisley. After a hundred yards look out for a big yellow sign post on the left indicating a path, which leads to the edge of the wood, where a small bridge heralds open country by a stile.

Head up the field obliquely for the large sycamore on the skyline. Looking back you will see you have indeed come through the more interesting deciduous part of the wood.

Flakebridge Wood bluebells

Just to the right of the sycamore, cross a barred gap style and carry straight on, aiming just to the right of the telegraph pole where another stile awaits you. Carry on alongside the wall marking the wood boundary on your left and follow the sign at the end going left down to the Keisley Beck and a bridge, with some stepping stones to help you over the bog.

Over the bridge, follow the path on the bank above marshy ground round to the wall. Follow this till a sign indicates you through the wall at a barred gap stile. Go straight up the field to a green lane which joins the minor road to Dufton.

Go right and then a quick left up the track to Keisley House, signposted High Cup Nick via Bow Hall. Go through a gate on the left before the house on a path leading to Town Head. Note the small vineyard on the left. Follow the signs, which take you to the right (north) of the buildings, and where a gate on the left indicates it is High Cup Wines, I strongly recommend you go through it and experience the free wine tasting in the converted barn visitor centre.

High Cup Winery

Opened in 2007 by Ron and Angela Barker, it produces eight fruit wines from their own fruit, plus extra from local growers, including grape vine in "good years" (last one 2006!). They are of good quality and worth tasting, even if you don't want to carry a bottle or two round the fells. It is Cumbria's only winery and vineyard. There is an excellent geological display explaining what you are about to see, and in July and August light refreshments and an art gallery of local scenes. Nominally open from 11 till 5, Thursday to Sunday, but if you ring the bell outside these times and the hosts are at home they will oblige you. Note that you could spend some time here, and that it is about an hour and a half so far from Appleby.

Refreshed, educated (or at least armed with a brochure about the Whin Sill), get back to the grassy track and follow it round, noting Dufton Pike and Bow Hall in the distance, past some boggy ground and over a little bridge. Here you can carry straight on, but if it has been wet so far it is less so to turn right through a gate just past the small bridge onto a quarry track, grassy and walled on both sides, which leads past the disused and unusual quarry of volcanic rock on the right side and onto the PW further up.

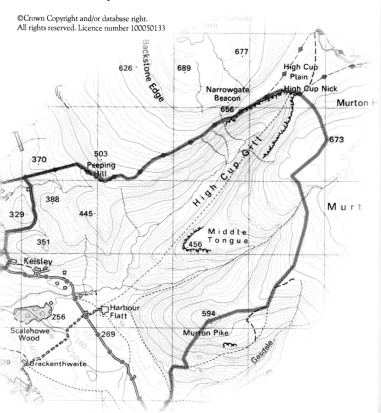

Turn right onto the broad track and continue climbing at an easy gradient, easily followed with many cairns past the last wall, except where the latter is passed through. Here, at NY722250, you can pass through two metal gates, or take a single wooden one on the left. The single gate leads via an oblique path to join the track later on past a lime-kiln.

As you approach the defile on your right the dolerite columns of High Cup Scar can be seen across it, a magnificent sight. Except in mist. See the section on geology at the start of the book for explanation. At the Nick, after perhaps descending a little to take a closer look at the columns on either side, return upwards and turn right, southeastwards, heading for the gully with a stream in it which splits the steep bank ahead. You are now in "Area Victor".

> **Area Victor**
> This is part of the Warcop Training Area for the army, but unlike the restricted area to the east, where firing, live and blank, takes place, this is called a "dry training" area, and no firing takes place. You may see men hiding, running, or doing whatever dry training really is. Or you may not. This is open access land and you are here by right. For more information see www.access.mod.uk.

Ascend the gully on its right side and keep on, heading for the curricks or big cairns as they are called round here, which you should eventually see on the northern summit of Murton Fell.

You will pass a bridleway, possibly by a signpost, heading southwest along the side of the hill, which you could follow, but to see the curricks carry on. There is no real path but the going is not hard underfoot.

At the cairns, either head south-west, the easy way, or, if a Nuttall/Hewitt bagger, plod over the moor to the cairn of Murton Fell. The easy way heads for a somewhat lesser cairn on the horizon:

a good quad track should soon appear to help you. If it peters out, head rightwards to pick up a bridleway with the occasional sign. This is mostly a quad track also, and leads to the cairn mentioned above. Carry on curving round to the left, southeast now to a further sign indicating a gate through a wall on the right. Do not go through this, but carry on by the wall till a nice cairned zig-zag path takes you down to cross Trundale Gill and up the bank to head south on a good path, joining a track by some shelters.

High Cup in winter

Pinnacle, High Cup Gill

At the "col" before Murton Pike, turn right off the track at a public footpath sign and ascend Murton Pike, quite steeply near the top, to be rewarded by a superb panorama: Great Dun Fell with its radar dome and towers to the north, with Cross Fell beyond; the Eden Valley with the Lake District hills beyond straight in front of you; the tent like Wild Boar Fell prominent to the south, with the wide mass of Baugh Fell beyond and to the right of it;

Murton Pike across High Cup Gill

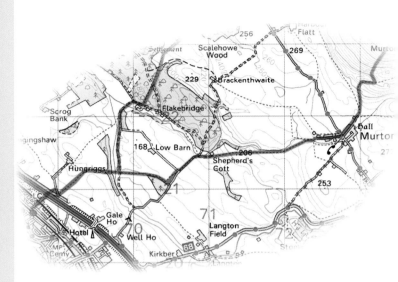

and Roman Fell to the southeast with the great wilderness of the Warcop Firing Range Fells "inland".

There is no path directly down from the summit, but the going is not rough, the least steep way being on a line somewhat to the right of Murton village, avoiding the steep descents to the hidden High and Low Troughs. Join the track again and through the car park (further geological board explanation) and go down the road through the pleasant village of Murton.

At the crossroads go half right, virtually straight across onto a residential road, which leads via a gate or stile at the end to a track past a water treatment works and a disused quarry. Note the footpath south of the beck is "unsafe", although actually only overgrown and muddy.

Past the quarry cross the beck by the footbridge and climb the bank diagonally to a gap stile in the wall, to carry on above, in order, the beck, wood and wall on the right. After crossing a wall and fence by stiles, take a line across the next field bisecting the angle made by the wall on your left and the plantation edge on your right, and aim to the left of Shepherd's Cottage when in view, trying to avoid the bog in front of it. The cottage track leads to a road; turn left here and turn right at the next track to the right, to Low Barn, and go immediately off that to the left on a footpath signposted to "Hungriggs". Follow the side of the field down to cross a fence stile and turn right along the bottom for about 600 yards till after a gate there is a crossroads of paths. Take the one straight on signed Appleby, into Stank Wood, and retrace your steps of several happy hours ago.

24. SCORDALE, LITTLE FELL AND ROMAN FELL CIRCULAR

Start and Finish: Appleby Station.
17.4 miles.   2839 ft. ascent.   8½ hours.
Summits: Little Fell, 2454ft., 748m.,(H,); Roman Fell, 1805ft., 594m.
Google Earth: reassures you of the existence and location of the pony track leaving the Roman Fell plateau. Bronze Age settlement not seen well.

Two things MUST be clearly understood before reading further.

FIRST: The hill part of this walk is on a live firing range, and you MUST NOT enter when live firing occurs, shown by red flags flying. Non-live firing is on twelve weekends per year (Google "Warcop Access Times"), after 1pm on Sundays, and at least 15 days and odd afternoons per year, with seven days notice, phone 0800-7835181 for details. This is updated daily.

SECOND: The MOD owns the land, and only wants you to use the rights of way on it. They think it is dangerous to stray off the paths and presumably do not want to be responsible for anything happening to you. The dangers are of unexploded shells and hidden mine shafts and are overstated: the area north and east of Roman Fell is not used much for firing, certainly not as much as it used to be, e.g. when training for the Falklands War in the 1980s, this land having similarities with the Falkland terrain. I think that previous descriptions of shells abounding here are now dated and that either the army has cleared up a lot or the shells have sunk in to the bog, hence all the signs not to dig! Hundreds of sheep are thought to be safe enough to graze here. The last time I did this walk I saw no shells, or mine shafts. Or humans. Do not touch any shells you may see.

The undertaking of this walk is therefore at your own risk. It is the longest walk in the book, but could be shortened by ascending one of the Augills from Scordale, or taking a car to Hilton. It has six miles of pathless moorland, but Scordale is continuously interesting. The whole area is usually deserted, I saw no-one in this wild and wonderful area one August bank holiday Saturday, and it is one of my favourite places, particularly Roman Fell.

From the north platform go down to the road and turn up it, to the right. As it curves to the right carry straight on a marked footpath, over a stile and across the busy A66 dual carriageway,

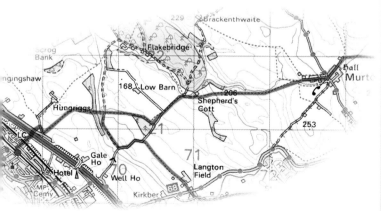

the Appleby bypass. There is an amusing stagger in the central reservation wires if you haven't the energy to step a foot over them. Across another stile into Roman Road, called so for obvious reasons, and straight on over another stile into a field, heading for a gate at the far end. Through this turn right into Hungriggs Lane, and just before it joins Roman Road go left over a stile into Stank Lane, a delightful path in spring but can be overgrown in summer, definitely not for shorts-clad legs then.

At the bottom go over a stile into a field, following its left side till the path swings diagonally right across it after 200 yards. Another stile is crossed at the far side and then in a

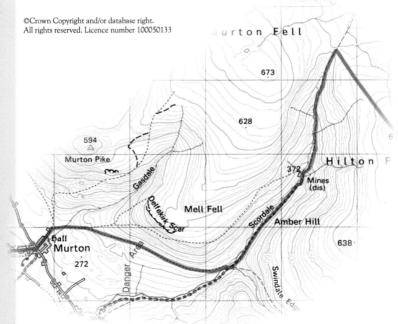

few yards another stile on the left leads into Stank Wood. A steep path leads through the wood, to cross a stile onto a grassy bank. Follow this to the signpost and straight on to "Murton" through a gate. The path heads along the bottom of the valley and shows the east spur of Roman Fell clearly ahead, which you will be descending much later.

Near the road at the end the path climbs the bank on the left and over a stile, to follow the right side of the next field. A stile at the end leads briefly to a track then right to the road. Turn left, and as it descends through some trees turn right over a cattle grid onto a track "Public Footpath Murton". The track goes to the right of the Shepherd's Cottage, then up the hill avoiding the bog as required, aiming for a telegraph pole with a yellow square on it. Now aim for the end of the plantation on the left, to cross a fence and wall by stiles, then follow the wall on the left then a wood and Murton Beck.

Roman Fell is clearly seen here over to the right, with the pony track, which is the key to your later descent, obvious on its right flank as it descends from the plateau.

A gap stile leads into a field and a post straight ahead indicates the way, but you don't need to climb to it, just head diagonally down to the beck to cross a bridge partially hidden by alders. Turn right up the track, over a gap stile past the water treatment works, and continue on up the road past mainly new houses to the crossroads. Note that the footpath south of the beck is "unsafe", although in my opinion it is merely muddy and overgrown.

Murton and Murton Pike

At the crossroads go straight

Scordale

Roman Fell from Upper Scordale

across and up to the car park. Take the footpath heading up right signed "White Mines, Scordale." A ladder stile leads over the next wall and the track fords a stream. At the next signpost take the right fork up the hill, the path here being vague, but over the next rise a useful marker is a stile with a white warning sign by it, by the wall under Delfekirk Scar. The left fork goes to this, but 250 yards down the hill from it your path goes through the wall by a gap stile not yet seen. The path, still intermittent, contours above a disused target wall, to pass through one more gap stile and after 300 yards descends to cross a wire fence by a stile just beyond the bridge. If you see two "do not dig here" signs before the descent, you have missed the path, return a little and descend to find it.

> ### Bronze Age settlement
> Note this is not marked on the map, but is centred on NY746213, between the beck and your path. It is a scheduled ancient monument and has been surveyed by English Heritage. A series of quadrangular fields marked by stone banks can be seen up close, and the bases of round houses. The climate was warmer and drier in the second millennium BC than it is now!

Cross the new bridge and go up Scordale by the track.

Scordale Mines

The entire valley from Swindale Brow up to above the waterfall is taken up by the remains of this mine, worked for galena (lead) from mediaeval times, but the hut ruins, tramways, slag heaps etc were from 1824 onwards, till 1876 for galena, then for barytes and witherite, sources of barium. Mining ceased in 1921 and when the MOD took over the land in the 1960s the mine entrances were sealed. Information boards exist up the valley.

The geology of the valley is basically similar to High Cup (see the geology section) with the Whin Sill dolerite appearing on the valley sides, but with more mineral rich veins (vertical, in cracks between the rocks) and flats, (horizontal).

The huge gash of Mason Holes can be ascended/descended safely but roughly, with more mossy saxifrage here than I've seen anywhere, and for those especially interested, there are guided tours, see the website www.keswickminingmuseum.co.uk.

The track climbs gently at first, and in the beck bed in one place, then more steeply after crossing the beck over a tunnel bridge above the main industrial remains. The bridleway is now on the left side of the beck, not as on the 2005 revised Explorer map. It is now marked with posts with permissive bridleway signs. The valley becomes intermittently dry as you are now in limestone terrain, and closes in.

At the watershed a post marks the highest point on the left of a boggy depression. Leave the path here and head by compass bearing up the ridge to Little Fell, which cannot be seen yet. A small rock on the horizon is a useful marker. The going is not too bad, but improved by a quad track and then, after some grit boulders and a cairn, an animal track which leads to the right side of the Little Fell ridge, then a human track left onto it about half way along. Large violets cheer you along in summer.

The summit is not defined. A path leads neatly round the south-western rim and across to the obvious shelter with trig point on the lesser summit of Burton Fell. The wilderness is impressive. Northeast is Mickle Fell, which used to be the highest hill in

Yorkshire, northwest the Radome on Great Dun Fell can be seen and then Cross Fell, across the wide Eden valley the northern Lake District fells, with Roman Fell in the near distance not so impressive from here. Further south Shap fells, the Howgills, and the Mallerstang valley are visible.

Mickle Fell from Little Fell

Continue towards a derelict metal box and tower, then a standing stone.

Head towards the watershed between you and Tinside Rigg/Roman Fell, a small path helping some of the way, to cross the bridleway marked with posts from Swindale to Lunedale, then head round or up Tinside Rigg on any animal paths you can find, watching for unexploded shells.

Scordale and Murton Pike from Christy Bank

Over some bare limestone the broad ridge leads to a col with an impressive line of shakeholes on the Roman Fell side. Go down this and up to the summit of Roman Fell for a full view of the Eden Valley with the Lake District hills beyond. The summit is marked by broken walls with a cairn inside, possibly an old building.

Pony track, Roman Fell

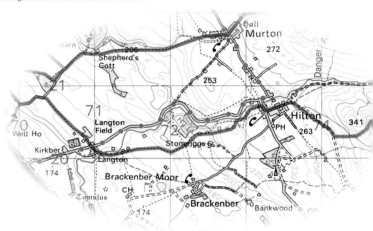

The key to a smooth exit off the Fell is finding where a definite old pony track leaves the plateau, at the western edge at NY755200. Go down the western rim of the fell till just before you are "opposite" the right angled corner of the walls below, and look around. It slopes diagonally down at a good gradient then eases off, here being a definite quad track, to contour and disappear. Keep contouring till the moor opens out, and descend the easy east spur to re-find the track just to the south of the quarry marked on the map. This leads down to an unfenced track, where turn right to gain the Hilton car park.

Go down the road through the main part of the village, which not surprisingly developed as a mining village, to the main B road and turn right. After fifty yards turn left by a footpath sign which takes you in front of a house. At the end a sign diverts you rightwards, to cross a gap stile on the left into a field and head down towards the beck. Down a bank a wall diverts you leftwards to a gate and stile, onto a green track, which climbs a bank above the beck, much pleasanter than taking the lower path through gorse bushes.

As you see Stoneriggs Farm, head right to go down and up a bank and continue to a signpost. Continue parallel to the wall on the right towards two tracts of water, through a gate in a slight depression, where the green track leads up to a signpost by a gap stile on the right. Go straight on however on the track, and as that veers away left, turn right on a thin path parallel to the wall. It leads above one of the golf fairways and down to pass by a golf green, and on towards Ellerholme, crossing another fairway.

At the track at Ellerholme turn left, then right past the barn to go by the Hilton Beck, some of the track having sunk into the beck recently. Over some naked red sandstone the path crosses the beck by a footbridge. Turn left and at the barn of Langton turn right through a gate and up through the farmyard to the Hilton road. Go straight across on the track "Public Footpath, Flakebridge Road". This passes by the cottages, through a gate, and alongside a long field. At Well House Road turn left, and over the rise turn right through a gate "Public Footpath", to pass along the valley and join your route of this morning at the four-pointing signpost. Remember to turn left to pass through Stank Wood and up Stank Lane.

The only blot on this long but superb outing is that there is no pub this side of the station, the Midland Hotel is just the other side! And note it is closed Mondays.

THE TOP TEN BEST:

1. **Flowers:** Smardale in June and July (and Greenriggs specifically for orchids).

2. **Skinny dip:** Baugh Fell, West Baugh Fell Tarn. Flat stones and total privacy.

3. **Wildlife:** Great Shunner Fell, the High Abbotside Moors.

4. **Limestone scenery:** Malham circular.

5. **Tarn:** Little Widdale Tarn, Great Knoutberry Hill and Widdale Fell.

6. **Industrial remains:** Scordale.

7. **Caves:** Victoria Cave, all the Attermire walks.

8. **Isolation:** Scordale, Little Fell and Roman Fell.

9. **Information:** The geological display at the Cumbria Winery, High Cup Nick and Murton Pike.

10. **Waterfall/slide:** Ewbank Scar, Nine Standards Rigg circular.